# Community Care and Control

## A Guide to the Legislation

## by Colin Fishwick

Copyright © Colin Fishwick 1992

ISBN  0 948680 25 3

**Dedication: To the memory of my parents**

# The Author

After studying for a law degree at Oxford University, Colin Fishwick took the Diploma in Social Administration at the London School of Economics. Training as a probation officer followed, and he practised as a probation officer in Nottinghamshire and Staffordshire. He moved to Birmingham Polytechnic to launch a new Probation Officer Training Course, which subsequently merged with other courses to become the Diploma in Social Work, of which he was Course Director for several years. He is currently Head of Social Work at the Polytechnic.

Colin Fishwick is also the author of 'Court Work: A Guide for Social Work practitioners' (Second Edition), 1989, and 'General law for Social Workers', 1988. This book completes his 'trilogy' of the substantive legal information required by probation officers, social workers and other care workers in their day-to-day practice.

**Date of Compilation - December 1991**

# Acknowledgements

The opportunity to devote a concentrated period of time to the preparation of this book was facilitated by my Head of Department, Professor Paul Waddington. I am grateful to him. Two other colleagues from the Polytechnic kindly read drafts and made useful suggestions for amendments. They are Helen Gorman, a social work lecturer and magistrate and a former Approved Social Worker, and Ann Ramsay, a law lecturer who specialises in family law. Their support and encouragement is appreciated.

Two solicitors with experience of working in the public sector, and currently legal advisers to the West Midlands Probation Committee readily undertook to scrutinise drafts and I thank them for their help. They are Richard Steer and Jean Marshall. A friend and former colleague, Peter Woolliscroft, Clerk to the Justices of Burton, Tamworth and Lichfield, generously agreed to bring a court clerk's perspective to what I had written and I am pleased to acknowledge it.

Fiona More worked with remarkable speed, efficiency and good humour in reproducing the material on the word processor. Nothing would have appeared without her efforts. Finally, I wish to thank Willie More of PEPAR Publications for his wise advice and assistance.

Without all this valuable help the book, which had to be prepared rather quickly, would not have been produced. What has been produced is intended to be helpful. If it fails in this main mission or in any other respect, I must accept responsibility.

*Colin Fishwick*                                                    *January 1992*

# Contents Guide

# Chapter Three - The Care and Control of People with Problems of Mental Health

# Chapter Four - The Care and Control of Offenders in the Community

# Preface

This book is published at a point in time when three major pieces of legislation are being introduced into the law relating to social welfare. The Children Act 1989 is expected to provide the framework for child care law well into the twenty-first century, and is now implemented. The National Health Service and Community Care Act 1990 is in the process of full implementation and reflects the approach to welfare services to adults that has come to be regarded as appropriate for society as the millennium ends. The Criminal Justice Act 1991, to be implemented in October 1992, offers a further attempt in this final decade of the twentieth century to make an appropriate response to offenders and their behaviour.

It is judged, therefore, an appropriate time to draw together this new legislation in one book, along with relevant existing legislation, to present the overall statutory framework of social welfare law.

This range of law comprises the essential components of social worker's and probation officer's professional law, that is the law relating to professional practice in various agencies and to the individual client. Having changed so dramatically, it is hoped that this compilation of the key elements of their professional law will be of assistance to experienced practitioners and social work students alike. It is aimed at being particularly helpful to students on the new DipSW courses, who are required to have competence in the areas of law on which social work practice is based.

However, the spirit of the recent legislation makes it inappropriate to present the law as though it were social workers' law, for it is the partnership between the professionals and the service users that is a key feature of much of the modern legislation. The emphasis on what citizens can expect under the provisions of this legislation means that the book has been written from that perspective also; hence, hopefully, it will be of use to clients and carers as well as professional practitioners.

Most interventions by social workers and allied professionals into the lives of citizens derive from statute and indeed those professionals are themselves the creation of statute. The value of such professionals embody altruism, caring for others and the drive to maximise people's potential and opportunities and to improve social conditions. But they are also the means by which society manages deviance from what are assumed to be agreed norms of behaviour. Such professionals find themselves, therefore, with caring and controlling functions, and constantly operating between individuals' needs and society's needs. While it is comfortable and crisp to speak of 'community care', it is perhaps more accurate – especially when it comes to the law – to speak of community care and control. It is for this reason that the focus of this book is the Law of Community Care and Control.

Because this volume is primarily based around new legislation, no case law is included. It is to be anticipated that before long there will be decisions made by the courts which will provide important inter-pretations of the statutes. Commentators have already identified potential confusions in the law as set down by Parliament, and the development of the law by the courts will need to be borne in mind as the legislation set out in these pages is progressively implemented.

Following the normal practice of legislation, the masculine gender is employed throughout and should be read as including the feminine.

# Chapter One

# The Care and Control of Children in the Community

## Introduction

The 1980s was a period of major review for child care legislation. The legislation prior to that time had become something of a tangled thicket, subject to much criticism, with various interlocking Acts and partial or amended implementations of them, making the whole area one of confusion and complaint. Added to this were changing patterns of child care practice, various child care scandals and developing social situations and values in respect of children and families.

The outcome of this period of review was a major piece of legislation, the Children Act 1989, which it is anticipated will shape the legal framework for child care for many years to come. The Children Act introduced a new legal concept – the concept of 'parental responsibility' – and established particular emphases and approaches in both the private and public law relating to children. The key principles underlying the Act are:

- children are generally best looked after within the family, with both parents playing a full role and without resort to legal proceedings: having parental responsibility;

- there should be local authority support for children and families in need, carried out in partnership, not substituting for the family;

- where parental responsibility has to be transferred, it should only be done by court order, and in the interests of the child;

- there should be full representation in any necessary court proceedings;

- any emergency powers should be of short duration and subject to challenge;

- when a child necessarily has to live away from home there should be clear-cut responsibilities for his care;

- provision for disabled children should be integrated into the overall framework;

- there should be flexibility between the private and public law.

This chapter, therefore, begins with a consideration of parental responsibility, guardianship and wardship of children. It moves on to local authority support of children and families with a consideration of the pivotal part of the Act – Part III – followed by childminding and other private services for children. Next, it considers court orders in respect of children in families facing change, before looking specifically at Supervision Orders and Care Orders and what is involved when there is more radical intervention in looking after children. The law governing the powerful interventions possible for the emergency protection of children at risk is covered before the chapter concludes with the ultimate long-term placement, adoption.

Young offenders are not included in this chapter, but are considered in Chapter 4, along with adult offenders.

All references in this chapter are to the Children Act 1989 unless otherwise stated.

## 1. Parental Responsibility, Guardianship and Wardship

### 1.1 Parental Responsibility

1.1.1　Part I of the Children Act 1989 introduces a new and fundamental concept into the law relating to children – the concept of 'parental responsibility'. Parental responsibility means all the rights, duties, powers, responsibilities and authority which by law a parent of a child has in relation to the child and his property (Section 3(1)).

1.1.2　Thus this definition refers to the legal relationship between a child and those concerned with his upbringing and care and decisions in respect of him, but does not affect the relationship of parent and child for other purposes. Therefore, parental responsibility can rest with various people, and can apply to a body, such as a local authority, as well as to an individual. Having or not having parental responsibility does not affect any obligation towards a

10

child which a 'parent' may have, such as a statutory duty to maintain him, nor does it affect rights of succession (Section 3(4)).

1.1.3　A mother of a child is consequently a parent who will always have parental responsibility, whereas a father is a parent who may have parental responsibility if he was married to the mother at the time of the birth of the child or at any time since conception and so is in law the father of the child by virtue of Section 1(2) and (4) of the Family Law Reform Act 1987. If not married to the mother, even though he may be the biological father, if he wants parental responsibility he will have to acquire it by due process (see 1.1.4 below). An unmarried father who does not have parental responsibility, being a parent for the purposes of the Act, has the right of any other parent to apply to the courts for any type of order and is entitled to reasonable contact with a child in care. He is not, however, entitled to remove a child from accommodation provided under Section 20, nor is his agreement required to the child's adoption (Section 10(4) and 34(1)). Any person who does not have parental responsibility but has care of a child may nonetheless do what is reasonable in all the circumstances of the case for the purpose of safeguarding or promoting the child's welfare (Section 3(5)).

1.1.4　An unmarried father may acquire parental responsibility

• by applying to the court for a parental responsibility order under Section 4(1),

• by having a residence order made in his favour (see below paragraph 5.5.8),

• by entering into a parental responsibility agreement with the mother under Section 4(1) which must be registered with the court in the prescribed manner,

• by being appointed guardian, either by the mother or by a court, to assume parental responsibility after the mother's death.

1.1.5 While a person with parental responsibility cannot surrender or transfer any part of that responsibility to another person, they may delegate responsibility on a temporary basis, such as to a babysitter or for a school trip, but it remains the duty of the person with parental responsibility to ensure that the arrangements are satisfactory. Otherwise, the person may be guilty of an offence under Section 1 of the Children and Young Persons Act 1933. (Section 2(9), (10) and (11))

## 1.2 Guardianship

1.2.1 The object of guardianship is to provide someone to take parental responsibility for a child whose parents have died. All guardians are non-parents, apart from those cases where an unmarried father is appointed guardian. A guardian is an individual person, not a body such as a local authority or voluntary organisation (Section 5(1)).

1.2.2 A guardian has the same parental responsibility as a natural parent (Section 5(6)).

1.2.3 A guardian may be appointed by

- any parent with parental responsibility,
- any guardian (to take his place as the child's guardian in the event of his death),
- a court.

1.2.4 A private appointment of a guardian will be valid in a will or provided it is in writing, is dated and is signed by the person making the appointment, or by another person in the presence of that person and two witnesses. A court can appoint a guardian either on application or of its own motion in any family proceedings (Section 5(5), 5(1) and 5(2)).

1.2.5 A court may appoint a guardian only

- where the child has no parent with parental responsibility for him (either because both parents have died or because his mother has died and his father does not have parental responsibility); or

- where the child still has a parent with parental responsibility, but there was a residence order in force in favour of a parent or guardian who has died, but not also in favour of the surviving parent (Section 5(9)).

1.2.6 A private appointment of a guardian – though made at any time – may only take effect in the same circumstances as above in which a court may make an order (Section 5(7) and (9)).

1.2.7 Any later private appointment revokes an earlier one unless it is clear that the purpose was to appoint an additional rather than a substitute guardian. Any appointment in a will is revoked if the will itself is revoked. A private appointment may also be revoked by the person who made it doing so in a written and dated instrument, signed by him or at his direction in his presence and that of two witnesses. An appointment made in a document other than a will can be revoked by destroying the document with the intention of revoking the appointment (Section 6(1), (2), (3) and (4)).

1.2.8 A privately appointed guardian may disclaim his appointment by written instrument, signed by him and made within a reasonable time of his first knowing that the appointment has taken effect. This disclaimer must be recorded in accordance with any regulations made by the Lord Chancellor (Section 6(5) and (6)).

1.2.9 Guardianship comes to an end automatically when the child reaches the age of eighteen, and any appointment may be brought to an end by order of the court on application by

- any person, including a local authority, who has parental responsibility for the child,

- the child himself, with leave of the court to apply,

or by the court's own motion in family proceedings (Section 91(7) and (8) and Section 6(7)).

## 1.3 Wardship

1.3.1 Wardship is not a creation of statute, but arises from the royal prerogative that the sovereign is under an obligation to protect all her subjects. It is, therefore, part of the inherent jurisdiction of the High Court. The Children Act 1989 has incorporated many of the beneficial features of wardship into statute, with its 'open door' policy and its flexible range of orders, with the aim of reducing the need to have recourse to the High Court. The inherent jurisdiction remains available as a remedy of last resort, but there is in the Act a specific prohibition against using the inherent jurisdiction in general, and wardship in particular, as an alternative to public law orders.

1.3.2 Thus, a local authority must have the High Court's leave to apply for the exercise of its inherent jurisdiction and leave may only be granted where the court is satisfied that the result which the authority wish to achieve could not be achieved through the making of any other order for which it can apply, and that there is reasonable cause to believe that if the court's inherent jurisdiction is not exercised the child is likely to suffer significant harm (Section 100(3), (4) and (5)).

1.3.3 Where a child is in care, the local authority has parental responsibility and should be able to take whatever decisions are necessary. The Act therefore makes wardship and care incompatible, and hence while a child is in care he cannot be made a ward of court and if a ward of court is committed to care the wardship ceases to have effect. The fact that decisions about children in care should be taken in consultation with parents and after taking the child's views into account should reduce the need for recourse to the High Court, but where this occurs, the Act prevents the court, in making an order under its inherent jurisdiction, from conferring on the local authority any degree of parental responsibility it does not already have (Section 100(2) and 91(4)).

14

1.3.4 Anyone, however, with a particular interest in a child or a blood-tie, or with whom the child has his home, or the child himself can make an application for wardship. A child is made a ward of court simply by completing a form called the originating summons filed in the Principal Registry or District Registry of the High Court. The child is a ward from the moment of application but remains a ward for only twenty-one days unless the wardship is confirmed by an order.

1.3.5 A child who is made a ward of court is in the legal protection and guardianship of the court, and all matters of importance relating to the ward's person and property should be referred to the court, as it is for the court to decide all serious issues relating to the child.

1.3.6 Within the twenty-one days of the originating summons, the applicant must issue a summons for directions for trial, which usually takes place at a preliminary hearing before a District Judge, but urgent or difficult cases can go directly to a High Court judge. At this hearing the arguments for or against continuing the wardship will be heard and directions given on the way the case is to proceed. Requests for urgent orders may also be heard at the preliminary hearing. At the substantive hearing all matters relating to the welfare of the ward will be considered; evidence is by affidavit, normally filed in advance, and then supported or challenged by oral evidence and cross-examination of witnesses in court.

1.3.7 Appeals against the decision of a District Judge (in the preliminary hearing) can be made to a judge in chambers, who will rehear the matter; appeals against the orders of a judge made at the substantive hearing can be made to the Court of Appeal.

## 2. Local Authority Support for Children and Families

### 2.1 General Duty

Section 17 of Part III lays a general duty on local authorities

* to safeguard and promote the welfare of children in need;

* as far as is consistent with that duty, to promote the upbringing of such children in their families by providing a range and level of services appropriate to those children's needs.

### 2.2 Children in Need

Local authorities do not, therefore, have to provide services for all children but only for those 'in need'. For the purposes of Part III a child shall be taken to be in need if:

* he is unlikely to achieve or maintain, or to have the opportunity of achieving or maintaining, a reasonable standard of health or development without the provision for him of services;

* his health or development is likely to be significantly impaired, or further impaired, without the provision for him of such services; or

* he is disabled (Section 17(10));

  For the purposes of this Part;

  – a child is disabled if he is blind, deaf or dumb or suffers from mental disorder of any kind or is substantially and permanently handicapped by illness, injury or congenital deformity or such other disability as may be prescribed;

  – 'development' means physical, intellectual, emotional, social or behavioural development;

  – 'health' means physical or mental health (Section 17(11)).

### 2.3 Support of Families of Children in Need

The services have to be provided to safeguard and promote the child's welfare, but they do not have to be provided directly to the child. (Section 17(3)).

16

'Family' includes any person who has parental responsibility for the child and any other person with whom he has been living (Section 17(10)).

## 2.4 The Services Provided

Every local authority must take reasonable steps to identify the extent to which there are children in need within their area and must publish information about the services provided (and where they consider it appropriate about the provision of services by others, in particular voluntary organisations) and take such steps as are reasonably practicable to ensure that those who might benefit from the services receive the information relevant to them (Schedule 2, Paragraphs 1(1) and (2)).

### 2.4.1 General duties

Through the provision of services under Part III of the Act local authorities have general duties to take reasonable steps designed:

- to prevent children suffering ill-treatment or neglect;

- to reduce the need to bring proceedings for care or supervision orders, criminal proceedings or any other proceedings which might lead to children being placed in the authority's care;

- to encourage children not to commit criminal offences;

- to avoid the need for children to be placed in secure accommodation. (Schedule 2, Paragraph 4(1) and 7)

### 2.4.2 Specific Services

- Every local authority must provide services designed to minimise the effect on disabled children of their disabilities and to give such children the opportunity to lead lives which are as normal as possible (Schedule 2, Paragraph 6).

- Every local authority must make such provision as they consider appropriate for children in need while they are living with their families to have available

17

- advice, guidance and counselling

- occupational, social, cultural or recreational activities

- home help (which may include laundry facilities)

- facilities for, or assistance with, travelling to and from home for the purpose of taking advantage of services under the Act or any similar service

- assistance to enable the child and his family to have a holiday (Schedule 2, Paragraph 8).

• Every local authority must provide such family centres as they consider appropriate (Schedule 2, Paragraph 9).

• Every local authority must provide such day care for children in need who are aged five or under and not yet attending schools, as is appropriate (Section 18(1)).

• Every local authority must provide for children in need who are attending any school such care or supervised activities as is appropriate outside school hours or during school holidays (Section 18(5)).

• Every local authority must provide accommodation for any child in need within their area who appears to require accommodation as a result of

- there being no person who has parental responsibility for him

- his being lost or having been abandoned

- the person who has been caring for him being prevented for whatever reason from providing him with suitable accommodation or care (Section 20(1))

- but, before providing accommodation, the local authority shall, so far as is reasonably practicable and consistent with the child's welfare, ascertain the child's wishes and give due consideration to them (Section 20(6))

- a local authority may not provide accommodation if any person who has parental responsibility for the child, and who is willing and able to provide or arrange accommodation for him, objects (Section 20(7))

- any person who has parental responsibility may at any time remove the child from accommodation provided by or on behalf of the local authority (Section 20(8)).

- Every local authority must make provision for the reception and accommodation of children who are removed or kept away from home under the provisions of Part V of the Act for the protection of children (Section 21(1)).

- Every local authority must receive and provide accommodation for children in police protection, remanded under the Children and Young Persons Act 1969, or requested to be received under the Police and Criminal Evidence Act 1984 (Section 21 (2)).

### 2.4.3 Possible Services

- The services provided by a local authority in the exercise of functions conferred on it by Section 17 of the Act – many of those above – may include giving assistance in kind or, in exceptional circumstances, in cash (Section 17(6)).

  - Assistance may be unconditional or subject to conditions as to repayment, but must have regard to the means of the child and of each of his parents, and no person shall be liable to any repayment if he is in receipt of income support or family credit (Section 17(7), (8), (9)).

- A local authority may provide day care for children aged five or under and not yet attending school even though they are not in need (Section 18(2)).

19

- A local authority may provide care or supervised activities for children within their area who are attending any school even though those children are not in need (Section 18(6)).

- A local authority may provide accommodation for any child within their area (even though a person who has parental responsibility for him is able to provide him with accommodation) if they consider that to do so would safeguard or promote the child's welfare (Section 20(4)).

- A local authority may provide accommodation for any person who has reached the age of sixteen but is under twenty-one in any community home which takes children who have reached the age of sixteen if they consider that to do so would safeguard or promote his welfare (Section 20(5)).

## 2.5 Recoupment of Cost of Providing Services

2.5.1 Advice, guidance and counselling is provided free of charge (Section 29(1)).

2.5.2 Where a local authority provides any other service under Sections 17 or 18 they may recover such charge for the service as they consider reasonable from

- each of his parents where the service is provided for a child under sixteen

- the child himself who has reached the age of sixteen

- the member of the family, where the service is provided for that member of the child's family (Section 29(1) and (4)).

2.5.3 Where the authority are satisfied that the person's means are insufficient for it to be reasonably practicable for him to pay the charge, they shall not require him to pay more than he can reasonably be expected to pay (Section 29(2)).

2.5.4 No person shall be liable to pay any charge while he is in receipt of income support or family credit (Section 29(3)).

2.5.5　Part III of Schedule 2 makes provision in connection with contributions towards the maintenance of children who are being looked after by local authorities and consists of the re-enactment with modifications of provisions in Part V of the Child Care Act 1980.

## 2.6 Co-operation between Authorities

2.6.1　The various powers and duties relating to children in need or being looked after are laid on the 'local authority' as a corporate body, but Paragraph 26 of Schedule 13 indicates that in this context 'the local authority' means the Social Services Department.

2.6.2　Section 27 lays a duty on certain other authorities to co-operate with the Social Services Department. The Department may request the help of that other authority or person, who shall comply with the request if it is compatible with their own statutory or other duties and obligations and does not unduly prejudice the discharge of any of their functions (Section 27(1) and (2)).

2.6.3　The persons are:
- any local authority
- any local education authority
- any local housing authority
- any health authority
- any person authorised by the Secretary of State.

## 2.7 Services Provided by Voluntary Organisations and the Private Sector

2.7.1　Every local authority must facilitate the provision by others (including in particular voluntary organisations) of services which the authority have power to provide - under Sections 17, 18, 20, 23 and 24 - and may make such arrangements as they see fit for any person to act on their behalf in the provision of any such service (Section 17(5)).

2.7.2　The next section of this chapter considers in particular childminding and day care for young children, which is covered by Part X of the Children Act 1989.

# 3. Childminding and Day Care For Young Children

## 3.1 General

"Part III also introduces the review duty under which local authorities working with local education authorities are required to review and report on the day care services in their area used by children aged under eight. This new duty, the general duty to provide day care for children in need (Section 18) and the modernised registration system in Part X of the Act to regulate independent day care services and childminding used by children aged under eight give local authorities for the first time a clear function to oversee and co-ordinate these services. This is expected to result in more efficient use of existing services and coherent development of new ones, and in particular to take full account of the potential of the private and voluntary sectors." (1)   So states the Department of Health in Volume 2 of its Guidance and Regulations on the Children Act 1989. This volume gives detailed guidance on family support, day care and educational provisions for young children.

## 3.2 Day Care: Functions of Local Authorities and Development of Services

3.2.1   The Act gives local authorities the following duties and powers to provide, regulate and (with local education authorities) review day care services in their area:

- a general duty to provide day care services for children in need and in making such arrangements to have regard to the different racial groups in the area to which children belong (Section 18 and Schedule 2, Paragraph 11)

- a duty to regulate the private and voluntary day care sectors and childminders (Part X and Schedule 9)

- a duty to publish information about services provided by themselves and others and to ensure that this information  is received by those who might benefit from them (Schedule 2, Paragraph 1)

- social services departments and local education authorities have a duty jointly to conduct and publish a report on a review of day care provision used by under 8s in the area at least once every three years (Section 19(1), (2) and (6))

- a power to provide day care for children who are not in need (Section 18(2) and Schedule 2 paragraph 11)

- power to provide facilities such as training, advice, guidance and counselling for those caring for children in day care (including as a childminder) and for parents, or those with parental responsibility or looking after children, who accompany a child attending day care (Section 18(3) and (4)).

3.2.2 The Department of Health's guidance states that in "carrying out the regulatory function registration has to be a positive process, there to help the setting up of good quality services for families to use on an informed basis and with confidence ... Local authorities should therefore use this function in an enabling and facilitating way and seek to encourage developments." It goes on: "In each area there will be a wide range of providers involved in developing and running day care services – different departments in local authorities, other statutory bodies, voluntary organisations, self-help or community groups, volunteers, private companies, private individuals running a business or working as a childminder or nanny, and employers in the public and private sectors. The pattern, level and delivery of services should be worked out locally and the process should involve all interested parties who include those mentioned above and community interests, ethnic minority groups and parents, churches and other places of worship. The new review duty provides a useful framework within which to develop services." (2).

## 3.3 Registration of Day Care Services and Childminding

3.3.1 Every local authority must keep a register of

- persons who act as childminders on domestic premises within the authority's area,

23

- persons who provide day care for children under the age of eight on premises (other than domestic premises) within that area (Section 71(1)).

3.3.2 A person is a childminder if

- he looks after one or more children under the age of eight, for reward; and

- he spends a period of more than two hours in any day looking after children (Section 71(2)).

3.3.3 A person does not provide day care until the total period during which children are looked after exceeds two hours in any day (Section 71(2)).

3.3.4 A parent, relative, person with parental responsibility, a foster parent, or a person employed as a nanny looking after a child wholly or mainly in the home of the person employing her, does not act as a childminder (Section 71(4) and (5)).

3.3.5 The social services department has to be satisfied the person applying to register is a 'fit person', and that other people living or working on the premises are 'fit to be in the proximity of children under the age of eight' (Section 71(7) and (8)).

3.3.6 The local authority also has to satisfy itself about the fitness of the premises before granting registration (Section 71(11)). The Department of Health's guidance sets out lists of points to which the local authority should have regard in drawing up its criteria for suitable premises(3).

3.3.7 Section 72 (childminders) and Section 73 (day care providers) set out the requirements which local authorities must impose on a person's registration and with which the registered person must comply. Local authorities have discretion to impose other requirements which must not conflict with the mandatory requirements which relate to:

- numbers of children

- maintenance and safety of the premises and equipment

- maintenance of records

- notification of charges

- numbers of staff (day care providers only).

3.3.8   The Department of Health's guidance gives details on all aspects of registration. Paragraph 1 of Schedule 9 requires people applying for registration to do so in accordance with regulations made by the Secretary of State which include providing details about the people helping to look after children and those living or likely to be living on the particular premises. The application is to be accompanied by whatever registration fee is prescribed in regulations made by the Secretary of State. (Child Minding and Day Care (Applications and Registration) Regulations 1991, The Child Minding and Day Care (Registration and Inspection Fees) Regulations 1991 and The Child Minding and Day Care (Applications for Registration and Registration and Inspection Fees) (Amendment) Regulations 1991.)

3.3.9   The Act lays on local authorities a duty to inspect domestic premises in which registered childminders are working and non-domestic premises where day care for children aged under eight is being provided, at least once a year. They may also authorise someone to enter any premises in their area if they have reasonable cause to suspect that a child is being looked after by a childminder who is not registered or by an unregistered person providing day care in non-domestic premises. A person exercising these powers must, if required, produce some duly authenticated document showing his authority to do so (Section 76(1), (2) and (6)).

3.3.10   In certain circumstances, specified in Section 74, the local authority may cancel the registration of a childminder or person providing day care (Section 74(1) and (2)). In an emergency, where a child is suffering or is likely to suffer significant harm, the local authority has power to apply to the court to cancel a person's registration, to vary an imposed requirement or to remove or to impose a requirement (Section 75).

3.3.11  Where a local authority

- refuse registration

- cancel registration

- refuse consent to a person disqualified from registration (Schedule 2, Paragraph 2)

- impose, remove or vary any registration requirements

- refuse to grant an application for variation or removal of a requirement

it must give at least 14 days notice of their intention to do so and the reasons for it and give the applicant an opportunity to object.  If, after hearing the objections, they still decide to take the proposed action, they must send a notice in writing and the person then has the right of appeal to the court (Section 77).

3.3.12  It is an offence without reasonable excuse, to provide day care for children under eight unless properly registered (Section 78(1) and (2)).

3.3.13  Where a local authority believes that someone is acting as a childminder whilst unregistered, they may serve an 'enforcement notice' on the person concerned informing him of the requirement to register and saying that he must not look after children aged under eight for reward until he is registered. If the person contravenes the notice he is guilty of an offence (Section 78(3), (4) and (6)).

3.3.14  Any person who without reasonable excuse contravenes, or otherwise fails to comply with, any requirement imposed on him in the registration as a childminder or as a provider of day care shall be guilty of an offence (Section 78(8)).

26

3.3.15 The Department of Health has published, and disseminated to local authority managers and legal advisers, a report of a survey of practice under previous legislation concerning the registration of childminding and day care, which identifies pointers for effective implementation of Part X and Schedule 9 of the Children Act 1989. It is called 'Registration of Child Minding and Day Care: Using the Law to Improve Standards" (HMSO 1991).

## 4. Private Fostering and Registered Children's Homes

### 4.1 Private Fostering

4.1.1 In general, private foster children are those whose parents place them for more than 28 days by private arrangement with a family which is not related to the child, either with or without payment. To be privately fostered the child must

- be under sixteen or, if disabled, under eighteen (Section 66(1) and 66(4)),

- be cared for and accommodated by someone who is not his parent or a relative and has not got parental responsibility (Section 66(1)),

- not be being looked after by a local authority or on behalf of a voluntary organisation (Schedule 8, Paragraphs 1 and 2(c)),

- not living in premises on which a parent, a person with parental responsibility for him or a relative who has assumed responsibility for his care, is living (Schedule 8, Paragraph 2(1)(a)).

4.1.2 It is the duty of every local authority to satisfy themselves that the welfare of children who are privately fostered within their area is being satisfactorily safeguarded and promoted and to secure that such advice is given to those caring for them as appears to the authority to be needed (Section 67(1)).

4.1.3  Where a person authorised by a local authority to visit privately fostered children has reasonable cause to believe that a child is being privately fostered in premises within the authority's area or it is proposed to accommodate any such child, he may at any reasonable time inspect those premises and any child there. If required, the authorised person must produce some duly authenticated document showing his authority to exercise these powers (Section 67(3) and (4)).

4.1.4  If not satisfied that the welfare of any privately fostered child is being satisfactorily safeguarded and promoted, the local authority shall, unless they consider that it would not be in the best interests of the child, take such steps as are reasonably practicable to secure that the care and accommodation of the child is undertaken by

- his parent,
- any person who is not his parent but who has parental responsibility for him, or
- a relative of his,

and must consider the extent to which, if at all, they should exercise any of their functions under the Act (Section 67(5)).

4.1.5  The 'usual fostering limit' of three children is prescribed by Paragraphs 2 and 3 of Schedule 7. The local authority has power to impose requirements on private foster parents as to the number, age, and sex of children who may be fostered, the standard of the accommodation and equipment provided, arrangements with respect to health and safety and particular arrangements with respect to the provision of care (Schedule 8, Paragraph 6).

4.1.6  A proposal to foster a child privately must be notified to the local authority in whose area the fostering is to take place. Certain persons are to be disqualified from being private foster parents under regulations made by the Secretary of State and the local authority may impose a prohibition where it is of the opinion that:

28

- the person is not a suitable person to foster a child,

- the premises in which the child is to be accommodated are not suitable,

- it would be prejudicial to the welfare of the child for him to be accommodated by that person in those premises.

(Section 68 and 69, The Children (Private Arrangements for Fostering) Regulations 1991 and The Disqualification for Caring for Children Regulations 1991)

4.1.7  A person shall be guilty of an offence if

- being required under any provision under this Part of the Act to give notice or information,

  – he fails without reasonable excuse to give the notice within the time specified,

  – he fails without reasonable excuse to give the information within a reasonable time; or

  – he makes, or causes or procures another person to make any statement in the notice or information which he knows to be false or misleading,

- he refuses to allow a privately fostered child to be visited by a duly authorised officer of a local authority,

- he intentionally obstructs a duly authorised officer in the exercise of the power of inspection,

- he contravenes Section 68 (in respect of persons disqualified from being private foster parents),

- he fails without reasonable excuse to comply with any requirement imposed by a local authority,

- he accommodates a privately fostered child in any premises in contravention of a prohibition imposed by a local authority,

- he publishes an advertisement which contravenes Paragraph 10 of Schedule 8 (which requires the person's name and address to be given in any advertisement indicating that a person will undertake or arrange private fostering).

(Section 70(1))

4.1.8 A person who is under 21 and who was, but is no longer, privately fostered at any time after his sixteenth birthday qualifies for advice and assistance from the local authority in whose area he is. The local authority may, but is not required, to advise, assist and befriend such a person. Assistance may be in kind or, in exceptional circumstances, in cash, which could be conditional on repayment except where a person is in receipt of income support or family credit (Section 24(2), (4), (5), (6), (7) and (10)).

## 4.2 Registered Children's Homes

4.2.1 Part VIII of the Act covers registered children's homes, and for the purposes of this Part a 'children's home' means a home which provides (or usually provides or is intended to provide) care and accommodation for more than three children at any one time (Section 63(3)). Normal domestic arrangements, community homes, voluntary homes, residential care homes and nursing homes and schools are excluded from the definition, except that an independent school which provides accommodation for not more than fifty children is a children's home (Section 63(5) and (6)).

The three children rule links with the 'usual fostering limit'. Where there are less than four children in a home or the children are all siblings of each other, the arrangement will constitute fostering, if the other requirements are satisfied.

4.2.2 Thus, children's homes are essentially private sector homes run for profit, and these homes must be registered with the local authority (Section 63(1)). Detailed guidance in respect of residential care in various types of provision is given in Volume 4 of the Department of Health's series on the Children Act (4) and the Children's Homes Regulations 1991 apply to various types of homes. Part VI of the Regulations set out the procedure for registration and the kinds of requirements which must be satisfied before an application may be granted. The local authority may impose conditions, and the registration must be reviewed annually. Within the period of one month ending upon the anniversary of the registration, the registration authority must inspect the home and on at least one other occasion during the year. Registration may be cancelled at any time if the home is not being carried on in accordance with the relevant requirements. The local authority must give the applicant a chance to make representations before decisions are made about registration or conditions attaching to it. Appeals may be made to a Registered Homes Tribunal (Schedule 6).

4.2.3 A person disqualified from privately fostering a child may not carry on or be employed in a children's home without the consent of the local authority (Section 65(1) and (2)).

4.2.4 The Children's Homes Regulations 1991 govern the placement of children in children's homes, the conduct of the homes and the welfare of children living there (see below, paragraph 8.6). The local authority also have a duty to satisfy themselves that the person carrying on a children's home is satisfactorily safeguarding and promoting the welfare of children in the home. If the authority are not satisfied about the welfare of a child, then, as in the case of private fostering, they must take reasonable steps to secure that the care and accommodation of the child is undertaken by a parent, relative or other person who has parental responsibility and must consider whether to exercise their functions under the Act.

4.2.5 As for private fostering, a person who is under twenty-one and who has left a registered children's home after his sixteen birthday qualifies for advice and assistance from the local authority; additionally, if he leaves a registered children's home after his sixteenth birthday, the person carrying on the home must inform the local authority where he proposes to live (Section 24(2) and (12)).

## 5. Court Orders with Respect to Children in Families Facing Change

### 5.1 Introduction

5.1.1 This chapter began with the 'pivotal part' of the Children Act – Part III – and also considered childminding and day care for young children together with private fostering and registered children's homes, because central to the philosophy of the Act is the positive approach that parents will normally want to make the best arrangements possible for the care of their children, and that they should have a range of services available to them for this purpose. In providing services, as we have seen the local authority should support families, not take over from them, and should work in partnership with parents in a way that promotes family relationships. However, there are also circumstances where it is necessary to use legal processes to arrange for the care and control of particular children. Again the Children Act 1989 adopts a positive approach when it comes to family proceedings, and it is in respect of these proceedings that its philosophy is made explicit.

5.1.2 Section 1(1) of the Act states:

"When a court determines any question with respect to

(a) the upbringing of a child; or

(b) the administration of a child's property or the application of any income arising from it, the child's welfare shall be the court's paramount consideration."

5.1.3 Besides this 'paramountcy' principle, the Act also sets out other principles governing the approach to be taken by courts:

- the court shall have regard to the general principle that any delay is likely to prejudice the welfare of the child (Section 1(2))

- where a court is considering whether or not to make one or more orders under this Act with respect to a child, it shall not make the order or any of the orders unless it considers that doing so would be better for the child than making no order at all (Section 1(5)).

5.1.4 In all family proceedings, therefore, the welfare of the child is paramount, delay should normally be avoided and even if the grounds for an order are established it should only be made if it can be shown that it would be better for the child than not making one. When considering whether to make, vary or discharge a Section 8 order or orders under Part IV of the Act, (see below), the court must have regard in particular to the following, which has become known as the welfare checklist:

- the ascertainable wishes and feelings of the child concerned (considered in the light of his age and understanding)

- his physical, emotional and educational needs

- the likely effect on him of any change in his circumstances

- his age, sex, background and any characteristics of his which the court considers relevant

- any harm which he has suffered or is at risk of suffering

- how capable each of his parents, and any other person in relation to whom the court considers the question to be relevant, is of meeting his needs

- the range of powers available to the court under this Act in the proceedings in question (Section 1(3)).

It should be noted that the welfare checklist does not apply to Child Assessment Orders, Emergency Protection Orders, Recovery Orders and Family Assistance Orders (see below).

## 5.2 The Courts

5.2.1 The Children Act establishes a concurrent system of jurisdictions in new magistrates' family proceedings courts, county courts and the High Court for a wide range of family proceedings. It also brings together private law and public law relating to children. In practice most public law applications (those for care or supervision orders) will start in the magistrates' family proceedings court, but in certain circumstances they may be transferred to a higher court. The criteria for transfer are

• exceptional complexity, importance or gravity

• the need to consolidate with other proceedings

• urgency

(Section 92 and Schedule 11)

5.2.2 For the time being it will continue to be possible to exercise free choice about which court is used in private law cases.

5.2.3 There is a general right of appeal to the High Court against both the making of and the refusal to make any order.

## 5.3 Proceedings in the Courts

5.3.1 The Children Act 1989 creates a clear division between civil and criminal proceedings, and ends the mixed approach which characterised aspects of the law relating to children in need and young offenders under the Children and Young Persons Act 1969. (Section 90)

5.3.2 The civil nature of applications is emphasised and a non-adversarial approach is encouraged. The Department of Health's guidance puts it thus:

"The rules of court which regulate the proceedings across all three tiers of jurisdiction have been designed to promote a non-adversarial style in court. The complaint/summons procedure has been abandoned in favour of the commencement of proceedings by application. For the first time a directions appointment is introduced to both

34

public and private law proceedings as a preliminary hearing at which, among other matters, timetables can be set, a guardian ad litem appointed in certain specified proceedings and evidential matters likely to be agreed or in dispute identified. These preliminary hearings should serve to minimise delay and produce less adversarial conduct of cases in court.

To facilitate ease of transfer between different juris-dictional tiers and to encourage the preparation of documentary evidence and advance disclosure, applications for most public and private law orders will be by way of prescribed forms. Applicants will be required to give a considerable amount of information as to the nature of their case, the order and any accompanying directions sought and, where relevant, their future plans for the child." (5)

### 5.4 Welfare Reports

A court considering any question with respect to a child under the Children Act may ask a probation officer or a local authority to report to the court on any matter relating to the welfare of the child. The report may be made in writing or orally, as the court requires, and may include hearsay. The Lord Chancellor may make regulations specifying matters which, unless the court orders otherwise, must be dealt with in any report (Section 7(1), (2), (3) and (4)).

### 5.5 The Court Orders

5.5.1  The court orders which can be made under Part II of the Act are intended to provide a flexible range of orders that can be made into a package which will best suit the needs of a child.  They will be made principally in private family proceedings but they may also be made in care proceedings (see section 6 of this chapter).

5.5.2  The orders are created by Section 8 of the Act and are referred to as 'Section 8 orders'. They are defined by Section 8(1) as follows:

- **"a contact order"** means an order requiring the person with whom a child lives or is to live, to allow the child to visit or stay with the person named in the order, or for that person and the child otherwise to have contact with each other;

- **"a prohibited steps order"** means an order that no step which could be taken by a parent in meeting his parental responsibility for a child, and which is of a kind specified in the order, shall be taken by any person without the consent of the court;

- **"a residence order"** means an order settling the arrangements to be made as to the person with whom a child is to live;

- **"a specific issue order"** means an order giving directions for the purpose of determining a specific question which has arisen, or which may arise, in connection with any aspect of parental responsibility for a child.

5.5.3 Section 8 orders may be made on a separate application or in the course of family proceedings either on application or of the court's own motion. There are three basic categories of applicants

- people who may apply as of right for any Section 8 order, who are

  – parents (including unmarried fathers) and guardians

  – any person in whose favour a residence order is in force with respect to the child (Section 10(4)).

- people who may apply as of right for a residence or contact order, who are

  – any party to a marriage (whether or not subsisting) in relation to whom the child is a child of the family

  – any person with whom the child has lived for a period of at least three years

  – any person who has the consent of each of the persons in whose favour a residence order is in force

- any person who has the consent of the local authority if the child is in care

- any person in any other case who has the consent of each of those who have parental responsibility

(Section 10(5))

- anyone else, with the leave of the court, including the child himself if the court is satisfied that he has sufficient understanding (Section 10(7) and (8)).

5.5.4    Local authority foster parents are subject to the additional restriction that they cannot apply for leave to make an application for a Section 8 order with respect to a child they have fostered at any time within the past six months, unless they also have the consent of the local authority, or they are relatives of the child or the child has lived with them for at least three years preceding the application (Section 9(3)).

5.5.5.   A local authority may not in any circumstances apply for or be granted a residence or contact order (Section 9(2)). A local authority can acquire parental responsibility only by means of a care order. In order that a court's private law powers should not be used to interfere with a local authority's exercise of its statutory parental responsibilities, it is provided by Section 9(1) that no court shall make any Section 8 order with respect to a child in care, except a residence order. If a residence order is made in respect of a child in care, it has the effect of discharging the care order (Section 91(1)). Any issue relating to contact with a child in care should be dealt with under Section 34 (see later, the sections in this chapter on the Effect of a Care Order – paragraph 6.4 – and Looking After and Accommodating Children).

5.5.6    A court shall not make any Section 8 order, unless the circumstances are exceptional, once the child has reached the age of sixteen or which will have effect beyond his sixteenth birthday (Section 9(6) and (7)). No Section 8 order may continue beyond the child's eighteenth birthday (Section 91(11)).

5.5.7   If the court makes a residence order in favour of someone who does not have parental responsibility, that person will have parental responsibility for as long as the order is in force, but not the right to consent to or refuse consent to the child's adoption, freeing for adoption or the appointment of a guardian (Section 12(2) and (3)).

5.5.8   If the court makes a residence order in favour of the unmarried father of a child who does not have parental responsibility, the court must make an order under Section 4 giving him parental responsibility and this will continue – after the residence order – until it is specifically revoked (Section 12(1) and (4)).

5.5.9   While a residence order is in force, no person may cause the child to be known by a new surname or remove him from the United Kingdom for any period greater than one month without either the written consent of every person holding parental responsibility or the leave of the court (Section 13(1) and (2)).

5.5.10  Section 8 orders may be made on an interim basis as well as for the final determination of a case. Therefore, in any family proceedings one or more of the orders could be made to settle arrangements for a child while the case is being heard. At the close of the case, a final package of one or more orders could be put in place as a long-term arrangement. The court also has power to include directions about how a Section 8 order is to be carried into effect, to impose conditions to be complied with, to specify the period of the order or any provision contained in it and to make such incidental, supplemental or consequential provisions as it thinks fit (Section 11(3) and (7)).

5.5.11  The following are entitled to apply for variation or discharge of a Section 8 order

● anyone who is entitled to apply for a Section 8 order

● the person on whose application the original order was made

● if the order is a contact order, the person who is named in it (Section 10(6)).

5.5.12 Contact orders and residence orders made in respect of a child's parents lapse if the parents subsequently live together for a period of more than six months (Section 11(5) and (6)).

5.5.13 A 'Family Assistance Order' may be made in any family proceedings where the court has power to make an order under Part II of the Act. A Family Assistance Order can only be made by the court acting on its own motion, and can be made whether or not it actually makes any order. The aim of a Family Assistance Order is to provide short-term help to a family. The help may be directed more to the parents than the child, to assist with the problems associated with a family facing change.

5.5.14 A Family Assistance Order requires a probation officer or a local authority to advise, assist and (where appropriate) befriend any person named in the order. The persons who may be named in the order are

- any parent or guardian of the child

- any person with whom the child is living or in whose favour a contact order is in force

- the child himself.

The order may also require the named person or persons to notify their address to and allow visits from the officer concerned. The court must be satisfied that the circumstances of the case are exceptional. The consent of every person named in the order, except the child, must be obtained by the court. The order lasts for six months, but further orders can be made. When both a family assistance order and a Section 8 order are in force at the same time, the officer concerned may refer to the court the question whether the Section 8 order should be varied or discharged (Section 16(1), (2), (3), (4), (5) and (6)).

# 6. Care Orders and Supervision Orders

## 6.1 General Approach

6.1.1 Beyond the provision of services to children and families in need, and beyond the situation where legal processes have been necessary to determine the nature of the care and the relationships for children whose families have had to face change, there comes a point where the state itself must take responsibility for the care and supervision of children.

6.1.2 The Department of Health's guidance sets out the principles for civil care and supervision proceedings thus:

- "The first is that compulsory interventions in the care and upbringing of a child will be possible only by court order following proceedings ... in which the child, his parents and others who are connected with the child will be able to participate fully.

- Second, a care or supervision order will be sought only when there appears to be no better way of safeguarding and promoting the welfare of the child suffering, or likely to suffer, significant harm ...

- Third, there will be common grounds for making care or supervision orders irrespective of the route by which cases proceed. These will need to address present or prospective harm to the child and how this is occurring or may occur ...

- Fourth, there will be greater emphasis on representing the views, feelings and needs of the child in these proceedings. Guardians ad litem must now be appointed in most kinds of public law proceedings where statutory intervention is sought under the Act unless the court is satisfied that this is not necessary in order to safeguard the child's interests ...

- Fifth, when a care order is in force the local authority and parents share parental responsibility for the child subject to the authority's power to limit the exercise of such responsibility by the parents in order to safeguard the child's welfare, and to some specific limitations on the authority. The Act also establishes a presumption of reasonable parental contact with children in care, subject to court orders and limited local authority action in emergencies." (6)

6.1.3 Care proceedings are family proceedings, therefore the full range of orders, including Section 8 orders and the family assistance order, is available. This means that the court could make one or more Section 8 orders as an alternative to a care order or a supervision order, if it considered such an order better suited to the child's needs. It could also make one or more Section 8 orders as well as a supervision order. (But as noted above – in paragraph 5.5.5 – a local authority can acquire parental responsibility only by means of a care order, and if a residence order is made in respect of a child in care it has the effect of discharging the care order.) Similarly the making of a care order with respect to a child who is subject of any Section 8 order discharges that order (Section 91(2)).

6.1.4 Care and supervision orders are mutually exclusive; the making of a care order with respect to a child subject to a supervision order discharges that order (Section 91(3)).

## 6.2 Applications for Care and Supervision Orders

6.2.1 Only a local authority or authorised person (at present this means only the NSPCC) may apply for a care or supervision order (Section 31(1)).

6.2.2 The child must be under the age of seventeen or under sixteen if married, and the order ceases to have effect at age eighteen unless brought to an end earlier (Section 31(3) and 91(12)).

6.2.3 Rules of court require the local authority or authorised person applying for a care or supervision order to serve a copy of the application on all parties to the proceedings. The child and any person with parental responsibility will automatically have party status. Others may be joined to the proceedings as the court directs.

41

6.2.4 A separate application must be made on the prescribed form for each child. The form is designed to encourage advance disclosure of relevant evidence to the court and other parties. On receipt of the application the clerk of the court will consider whether the proceedings should be transferred to a higher court in accordance with the Allocation and Transfer Rules. A directions appointment may be held at any time during the course of the proceedings, and as the court will not usually be able to decide the application at the first hearing, the applicant should be ready to tell the court at the directions appointment:

- whether he is applying for an interim order, and if so, any directions with regard to the medical or psychiatric examination or other assessment of the child, which can be ordered under Section 38(6) where a court makes an interim care or supervision order. A child of sufficient understanding may refuse to submit to an examination or assessment.

- what plans the authority have made for safeguarding and promoting the child's welfare while the interim order is in force.

- in the case of an interim order, what proposals the authority have for allowing the child reasonable contact with his parents and others.

The court is required to draw up a timetable with a view to disposing of the application without delay, and to give such instructions as it considers appropriate for seeing that the timetable is adhered to (Section 32(1)).

6.2.5 Interim care orders and interim supervision orders can be made when a court adjourns proceedings hearing an application for a full care or supervision order or when, under Section 37(1), in other family proceedings, it appears that it may be appropriate for a care or supervision order to be made, and the court directs the appropriate authority to undertake an investigation of the child's circumstances (Section 38(1)).

42

6.2.6 The court has to be satisfied that there are reasonable grounds for believing that the criteria for a full care or supervision order are fulfilled before making an interim order, but, of course, the court requires proof of the criteria before making a full order (Section 38(2)).

6.2.7 A first interim order may last for up to 8 weeks, and a second or subsequent order may last for up to 4 weeks. There is no limit on the number of interim orders that can be made, but the emphasis should be on reaching a final hearing as quickly as possible (Section 38(4)).

## 6.3 Grounds for a Care or Supervision Order

6.3.1 A court may only make a care order or a supervision order if it is satisfied

- that the child concerned is suffering, or is likely to suffer, significant harm; and
- that the harm, or likelihood of harm is attributable to
  - the care given to the child, or likely to be given to him if the order were not made, not being what it would be reasonable to expect a parent to give him;
  - or the child's being beyond parental control (Section 31(2)).

6.3.2 If these conditions are met, the court may make an order, but it must apply the paramountcy principle (see page 30), consider the welfare checklist (see page 31) and operate on the presumption of no order (see page 31). It must also consider the wide range of powers available to it to make other orders and to give directions.

6.3.3 In respect of present or anticipated harm, the Act states:

- *"harm"* means "ill treatment or the impairment or development"
- *"development"* means "physical, intellectual, emotional, social or behavioural development"
- *"health"* means "physical or mental health"
- *"ill-treatment"* includes sexual abuse and forms of ill-treatment which are not physical (Section 31(9)).

6.3.4   The court must decide whether the harm is significant by comparing the health and development of the child concerned with that of a hypothetical similar child, where the question of whether the harm suffered turns on the child's health or development. It must also be satisfied that the harm or likelihood of harm is attributable to the care given or likely to be given to the child, and here the test is what a reasonable parent would give him, having regard to his needs.

## 6.4   The Effect of a Care Order

6.4.1   While a care order is in force the local authority have parental responsibility for the child and the power to determine the extent to which a parent or guardian may meet his or her responsibility for the child (Section 33(3)).

6.4.2   However, the power to determine a parent's or guardian's parental responsibility is limited in several ways:

- the authority may not exercise its power unless they are satisfied that it is necessary to do so in order to safeguard or promote the child's welfare

- the power shall not prevent a parent or guardian doing what is reasonable in all the circumstances for the purpose of safeguarding or promoting the child's welfare

- the authority may not cause the child to be brought up in any religious persuasion other than that in which he could have been brought up if the order had not been made

- the authority may not consent or refuse consent to the making of an application for adoption or agree or refuse to agree to an adoption order

- the authority may not appoint a guardian for the child

- no person may change the child's surname or remove him from the United Kingdom while a care order is in force, without either the written consent of every person who has parental responsibility for the child or the leave of the court. The removal does not apply where it is for less than a month (Section 33(5), (6) and (7)).

44

6.4.3   The local authority is responsible for 'looking after' the child (see section 8 of this chapter).

6.4.4   The parents or guardians of a child in care do not lose their parental responsibility on the making of a care order, but share it with the local authority, which can determine the extent of the parent's or guardian's responsibility, as stated above. The Department of Health's guidance states: "Where a local authority intend to limit the way in which a parent meets his responsibility this should be discussed with the parent and incorporated in the plan of arrangements for the child whilst in care so that it may be subject to periodic reviews." (7).

6.4.5   Parental contact and other contact is a key concept in the Children Act 1989, and is considered in section 8 (paragraph 8.7) of this chapter.  Where a child is in care the authority shall allow reasonable contact with

• his parents

• any guardian of his

• the person in favour of whom any residence order was in force immediately before the care order was made

• the person, if any, who had the care of the child by virtue of wardship immediately before the care order was made.

It is for the local authority to decide, subject to any court order, how much contact is reasonable.  The authority can refuse contact to those listed above only if they are satisfied that it is necessary to do so to safeguard or promote the child's welfare and the refusal is decided upon as a matter of urgency.  Such refusal cannot last for more than seven days (Section 34(1) and (6)).

6.4.6   The authority or the child may apply to the court for an order authorising the authority to refuse to allow contact between the child and any of the above persons named in the order (Section 34(4)).

6.4.7   Any of the people listed, or any other person with the leave of the court, may make an application to the court to make such order as it considers appropriate with respect to the contact which is to be allowed between the child and that person (Section 34(2)).

6.4.8   Before making a care order the court must consider the arrangements which the authority have made, or propose to make, for contact and must invite the parties to the proceedings to comment on them. The court may also vary or discharge any order made under Section 34 in respect of contact, on the application of the authority, the child, or the person named in the order (Section 34(11) and (9)).

6.4.9   Repeat applications for orders under Section 34 are controlled by Section 91(17) whereby a person who has had an application for an order refused may not reapply for the same order within six months without leave of the court.

6.4.10  From these provisions about contact, it can be seen, in the words of the Department of Health's guidance, that "The underlying principle is that the authority, child and other persons concerned should as far as possible agree reasonable arrangements before the care order is made, but should be able to seek the court's assistance if agreement cannot be reached or the authority want to deny contact to a person who is entitled to it under the Act." (8)

## 6.5 The Effects of a Supervision Order

6.5.1   A supervision order lays obligations on the supervisor and the child. It may also lay obligations on any person with parental responsibility or any other person with whom the child is living – called "the responsible person" in the Act. Detailed provisions in respect of supervision orders are set out in Parts I and II of Schedule 3 of the Act.

6.5.2   Subject to it being brought to an end earlier, a supervision order lasts for one year, but the supervisor can apply for

46

extensions up to a maximum of three years from the original date of the order (Schedule 6, Paragraph 6(1), (3) and (4)).

6.5.3   The supervision order designates the appropriate local authority, but the child may be placed under the supervision of a probation officer if the appropriate authority request and a probation officer is already exercising or has exercised, in relation to another member of the household to which the child belongs, duties imposed on probation officers under the Powers of the Criminal Courts Act 1973. (Schedule 6, Paragraph 9(1) and (2))

6.5.4   It is the duty of the supervisor to advise, assist and befriend the supervised child and to take such steps as are reasonably necessary to give effect to the order (Section 35(1)).

6.5.5   A supervision order may require the supervised child to comply with any directions given from time to time by the supervisor and requiring the child

- to live at a place or places specified in the directions for specified periods

- to present himself to any specified person at a place and on a day or days specified

- to participate in specified activities.

It shall be for the supervisor to decide whether and to what extent he exercises the power to give directions and to decide the form of any directions (Schedule 3, Paragraph 2).

6.5.6   The powers of the supervisor do not extend to giving directions in respect of medical or psychiatric examination or treatment, which are covered separately. A supervision order may require the child

- to submit to a medical or psychiatric examination

- to submit to any such examination from time to time as directed by the supervisor

- but no court shall include such a requirement unless satisfied, where the child has sufficient understanding to make an informed decision, he consents and satisfactory arrangements have been or can be made

- to submit to specified treatment for a mental condition or physical condition where conditions set out in Schedule 3, Paragraph 5 are met.

The same requirements regarding consent apply to treatment as apply to examination. The medical practitioner responsible for the treatment must make a report in writing to the supervisor if of the opinion that:

- the treatment should continue beyond the specified period

- the child needs different treatment

- the chile is not susceptible to treatment

- the child does not require further treatment

- he is unwilling to continue to treat the child

and the supervisor must refer the report to the court (Schedule 3, Paragraphs 4, 5 and 6).

6.5.7 With the consent of the 'responsible person', a supervision order may impose obligations on the responsible person by including a requirement

- that he take all reasonable steps to ensure that the supervised child complies with any directions given by the supervisor

- that he take all reasonable steps to ensure that the child complies with any requirement in respect of medical examination or treatment

- that he comply with any directions given by the supervisor requiring him to attend at a place specified for the purpose of taking part in specified activities (with or without the supervised child)

- that he keep the supervisor informed of his address if it differs from the child's (Schedule 3, Paragraph 3).

6.5.8   The supervision order may also require the child and the responsible person to keep the supervisor informed of any change in the child's address and to allow the supervisor to visit him at the place where he is living (Schedule 3, Paragraph 8).

6.5.9   The total number of days in respect of which a supervised child or a responsible person may be required to comply with directions as stated in paragraphs 6.5.5, 6.5.6 and 6.5.7 above shall not exceed 90 or such lesser number as specified in the order (Schedule 3, Paragraph 7).

## 6.6   Variation of Care and Supervision Orders

6.6.1   It is possible for a supervision order to be varied, but the Act does not provide for the variation of a care order, as the management of compulsory care is the local authority's responsibility. However, as noted above, there can be applications to the court to vary or discharge any order made in respect of contact with a child in care under Section 34, during the period of a care order. The court can also deal with an application for discharge of a care order by substituting a supervision order without having to re-establish the grounds for the order. But a care order can be made where a child was subject to a supervision order only after a fresh finding that the grounds for such an order are satisfied after a full hearing, even though the application may arise from non-compliance with the terms of the original supervision order (Section 39(2), (3), (4) and (5)).

6.6.2   An application for the variation of a supervision order may be made by

• any person having parental responsibility for the child

• the child

• the supervisor

and a person with whom the child is living (if not a person with parental responsibility) may apply for the order to be varied in so far as it imposes a requirement which affects that person (Section 39(2) and (3)).

49

6.6.3   It is the duty of the supervisor to consider whether or not to apply for the variation or discharge of a supervision order where

- the order is not wholly complied with, or

- the supervisor considers that the order may no longer be necessary (Section 35(1)).

6.6.4   The Department of Health's guidance advises: "The supervisor should ... review the need for, and reasonableness of, any directions he has given to the child or responsible person under the order, the arrangements made for carrying them out, and whether it would be in the interests of the child to change these. In considering whether to make applications to the court, he should consider how the court would be likely to view the application using the checklist in Section 1(3)." (9).

## 6.7   Discharge of Care and Supervision Orders

6.7.1   A care order may be discharged by the court on the application of

- any person having parental responsibility for the child

- the child

- the local authority designated by the order

and a supervision order on the application of

- any person who has parental responsibility for the child

- the child

- the supervisor

(Section 39(1) and (2))

6.7.2   The Review of Children's Cases Regulations 1991 requires the local authority to consider at least at every statutory review of a child in care whether to apply for the discharge of the care order. As part of the review, the child has to be informed of steps he himself may take, which include applying for discharge of the order.

6.7.3    As noted earlier – at 5.5.5 above – the only Section 8 order that can be made in respect of a child in care is a residence order, and such an order has the effect of discharging the care order. As part of the statutory reviews of a child in care, the child should also be told of his right to seek leave to apply for a residence order.

6.7.4    As will be seen in the later section of this chapter on 'Looking After and Accommodating Children', the care authority should work in suitable cases to enable the child to live with his parent(s), a person with parental responsibility for him, any person in whose favour a residence order was in force immediately before the care order was made, or a relative, friend or other person connected with him (Section 23(6)).

6.7.5    As noted above – at 6.6.3 – it is the duty of the supervisor to consider whether or not to apply for the discharge of a supervision order if the order is not complied with or is no longer necessary (Section 35(1)).

6.7.6    No further application may be made within six months without the leave of the court where a previous application for the discharge of a care order or a supervision order or the substitution of a supervision order for a care order has been dealt with (Section 91(15)).

## 6.8    Appeals Against Care and Supervision Orders

6.8.1    Anyone who had party status in the original proceedings (including the parents, child and local authority) may appeal against the making of a care or supervision order, or the varying or discharging of such an order or the court's refusal to make such an order.

6.8.2    Decisions by a magistrates' court are appealable to the High Court; decisions by a county court or High Court go to the Court of Appeal (Section 94(1) of the Children Act 1989 and Section 77(1) of the County Courts Act 1984 and Section 16 of the Supreme Court Act 1981).

6.8.3 Where there is already some compulsory intervention in the child's upbringing, the court can make orders intended to maintain continued protection or continuity of care for the child until the appeal is heard, as follows:

- where the court dismisses an application for a care order and the child is at that time subject to an interim care order, the court may make a care order pending appeal;

- where the court dismisses an application for a care order or a supervision order and the child is subject to an interim supervision order the court may make a supervision order pending appeal.

The court can, in these circumstances, include directions in the order on any matter to do with the child's welfare. Where the court agrees to discharge a care or supervision order, it may order that its decision shall not have effect, pending appeal; or that the order should remain in force subject to any directions it makes (Section 40(1), (2) and (3)).

6.8.4 These pending-appeal orders can be extended by an appeal court until the date the appeal is determined or, where no appeal is made, the expiry date during which an appeal can be made (Section 40(5) and (6)).

## 6.9 Referral to the Local Authority by the Court

6.9.1 As was noted earlier – paragraph 6.2.1 – only a local authority or authorised person may apply for a care or supervision order. However, where in any family proceedings in which a question arises about the welfare of any child, it appears to the court that it may be appropriate for a care or supervision order to be made, the court may direct the local authority to undertake an investigation of the child's circumstances (Section 37(1)).

6.9.2 Such a direction from the court requires the local authority to consider whether to take any action, such as applying for a care or supervision order or providing services or assistance to the child or his family. If the authority decide not to apply for a care or supervision order, they must report their decision to the court, giving the reasons and details of any action they are taking or proposing to take in respect of the child. This information must be provided within eight weeks unless the court directs otherwise. The local authority must also consider whether the child's circumstances should be reviewed at a later date and, if so, when that review should begin (Section 37(2), (3), (4) and (6)).

6.9.3 As will be seen below - at paragraph 7.4.2 - a court may also direct the local authority to investigate the circumstances of the child when it discharges an education supervision order.

## 7. Education Supervision Orders

### 7.1 Applications for Education Supervision Orders

7.1.1 Only the local education authority may apply for an education supervision order.

7.1.2 Where the authority propose to apply, they must first consult the social services department, in order to decide whether it would be appropriate for the local authority to provide services under Part III of the Act or to apply for a care or supervision order (Section 36(1) and (8)).

### 7.2 Grounds for an Education Supervision Order

7.2.1 A court may only make an education supervision order if it is satisfied that the child concerned is of compulsory school age and is not being properly educated (Section 36(3)).

7.2.2 A child is being properly educated only if he is receiving efficient full-time education suitable to his age, ability and aptitude and any special educational needs he may have (Section 36(4)).

7.2.3 Where a child is the subject of a school attendance order and it is not being complied with or is a registered pupil

53

at a school which he is not attending regularly (within the meaning of Section 39 of the Education Act 1944) then it shall be assumed that he is not being properly educated unless it is proved that he is (Section 36(5)).

## 7.3 The Effects of an Education Supervision Order

7.3.1 An education supervision order lasts for one year, but the local education authority may apply for an extension or extensions. Each extension may last for up to three years. An application for an extension may not be made earlier than three months before the date on which the order would otherwise expire. In any case the order ceases to have effect if a care order is made or the child ceases to be of compulsory school age (Schedule 3, Paragraph 15).

7.3.2 It is the duty of the supervisor to advise, assist and befriend, and give directions to the child and his parents in such a way as will, in his opinion, secure that the child will be properly educated (Schedule 3, Paragraph 12).

7.3.3 In giving directions, the supervisor must take into account the wishes and feelings of the child, having regard to his age and understanding, and of his parents, which it has been possible to ascertain (Schedule 3, Paragraph 12).

7.3.4 The order may require the child to keep the supervisor informed of his address and to allow the supervisor to visit him. It also requires a parent to inform the supervisor of the child's address (if known to him) and to allow reasonable contact with the child (Schedule 3, Paragraph 16).

7.3.5 Where a supervisor's directions are not complied with, he is under a duty to consider what further steps to take in the exercise of his powers. The options include

- making new directions
- referring the case to the local authority
- applying for discharge of the order

(Schedule 3, Paragraphs 12, 17 and 19)

54

7.3.6 The child's parents are required to comply with the supervisor's directions , and persistent failure to comply is an offence. It is a defence, however, if the parent can prove he took all reasonable steps to ensure that the direction was complied with, or the direction was unreasonable, or it was not reasonably practicable to comply with both a direction given under a ('ordinary') supervision order or a criminal supervision order and the education supervision order (see below – paragraph 7.4.3 – concurrent orders) (Schedule 3, Paragraph 18).

7.3.7 If the child persistently fails to comply with a direction, the local education authority must notify the local authority - in practice the social services department – who should investigate the child's circumstances (Schedule 3, Paragraph 19).

7.3.8 Parents lose the right to have the child educated in accordance with their wishes while an education supervision order is in force. They no longer have the right to move their child to another school and have no right of appeal against admissions decisions (Schedule 3, Paragraph 13).

## 7.4 Discharge of Education Supervision Orders

7.4.1 An application for the discharge of an education supervision order may be made by

- the child

- a parent of his

- the local education authority (Schedule 3, Paragraph 17)

7.4.2 On discharging the order the court may direct the local authority to investigate the circumstances of the child. The authority will then have to consider whether to provide services to the child or his family and whether an application should be made for some other order under the Act (Schedule 3, Paragraph 17).

7.4.3 An education supervision order may run concurrently with a supervision order or criminal supervision order. However, if an earlier criminal supervision order contained requirements as to the child's education, those requirements will cease to have effect when the education supervision order is made. An existing school attendance order is also discharged by the making of an education supervision order and a new one cannot be made (Schedule 3, Paragraph 13).

7.4.4 No further application may be made within six months without the leave of the court where a previous application for the discharge of an education supervision order has been dealt with (Section 91(15)).

# 8. Looking After and Accommodating Children

## 8.1 The Meaning of "Looking After"

8.1.1 A child is looked after by a local authority if he is

- in their care, or
- provided with accommodation by the authority in the exercise of their social services functions (Section 22(1)).

8.1.2 Accommodation means accommodation provided for a continuous period of more than 24 hours. In care means in care under a court order (Section 22(2)).

8.1.3 Thus 'looked after' children are those

- on a care order
- provided with accommodation by agreement with the parents or with the child if aged 16 or over
- accommodated away from home under an emergency protection order
- on remand
- under supervision with a residence requirement to live in local authority accommodation

56

- in police protection or arrested and at the police's request accommodated by the local authority

## 8.2 The Powers and Duties of the Local Authority

8.2.1  "One of the key principles of the Children Act", states the Department of Health's guidance, "is that responsible authorities should work in partnership with the parents of a child who is being looked after and also with the child himself, where he is of sufficient understanding, provided that this approach will not jeopardise his welfare." (10).

8.2.2  It is the duty of a local authority looking after any child

- to safeguard and promote his welfare; and

- to make such use of services available for children cared for by their own parents as appears reasonable in his case (Section 22(3)).

8.2.3  Before making any decision with respect to the child the local authority must, so far as is reasonably practicable, ascertain the wishes and feelings of

- the child

- his parents

- any other person who has parental responsibility for him

- any other person whose wishes and feelings the authority consider relevant (Section 22(4)).

8.2.4  In making any such decision, the local authority must give due consideration to

- such wishes and feelings of the child as they have been able to ascertain, having regard to his age and understanding

- such wishes and feelings of any other person mentioned above as they have been able to ascertain

- the child's religious persuasion, racial origin and cultural and linguistic background (Section 22(5)).

8.2.5     If it appears necessary, for the purpose of protecting members of the public from serious injury, to exercise their powers with respect to a child whom they are looking after in a manner that is not consistent with the above duties, then the local authority may do so (Section 22(6)).

8.2.6     It is the duty of any local authority looking after a child to provide him with accommodation and to maintain him in other respects by

- placing him with a family
- placing him with a relative
- placing him with any other suitable person
- maintaining him in a community home
- maintaining him in a voluntary home
- maintaining him in a registered children's home
- maintaining him in a home provided by the Secretary of State
- making other arrangements which seem appropriate and comply with any regulations made by the Secretary of State (Section 23(1) and (2)).

8.2.7     Part II of Schedule 2 of the Act sets out the regulation making powers in respect of children looked after by local authorities, which are detailed below, and adds the following duties and powers to those above which a local authority has in respect of children being looked after:

- a duty to promote contact between the child and his parents, any other person with parental responsibility and any relative, friend or other person connected with him, unless it is not reasonably practicable or consistent with his welfare;

- a duty to take such reasonable steps as are reasonably practicable to secure that his parents and any other person with parental responsibility are kept informed of where he is being accommodated;

58

- a power to make travelling, subsistence and other expenses to the child, the parents, any other person with parental responsibility, any relative, friend or other person connected with the child, for the purpose of visiting, where the circumstances warrant;

- a duty to appoint an independent visitor where communication between the child and his parents or other persons with parental responsibility is infrequent or he had not been to visit or been visited by them during the preceding twelve months. No such appointment shall be made if the child objects and has sufficient understanding to make an informed decision. (Schedule 2, Paragraphs 12, 13, 14, 15, 16 and 17)

8.2.8 It is also the duty of each responsible authority to review the case of each child while he is being looked after or provided with accommodation by them in accordance with the Review of Children's Cases Regulations 1991 (see below, paragraph 8.10).

8.2.9 As was noted earlier in the chapter – at paragraph 2.6 – there is a duty laid on various other authorities to co-operate with a social services department which is providing services to children in need or to children whom the local authority is looking after.

8.2.10 Part III of Schedule 2 sets out the provisions for contributions towards the maintenance of children looked after by local authorities.

An authority may only recover contributions where they consider it reasonable to do so, from

- each of his parents, where the child is under sixteen

- the child himself, where he has reached the age of sixteen.

A parent in receipt of income support or family credit is not liable to contribute, nor is any person liable during any period during which the child is allowed by the authority to live with a parent.

59

8.2.11 Where a child is being looked after by a local authority, it shall be the duty of the authority to advise, assist and befriend him with a view to promoting his welfare when he ceases to be looked after by them. They may also help a person qualifying for advice and assistance which is someone under twenty-one who was, at any time since reaching the age of sixteen

- looked after by a local authority
- accommodated by or on behalf of a voluntary organisation
- accommodated in a registered children's home
- accommodated by any health or education authority or in any residential care home, nursing home or mental home for a consecutive period of at least three months
- privately fostered

(Section 24(1) and (2))

## 8.3 Arrangements for the Placement of Children

8.3.1 The Children Act encourages certain types of placement, as follows:

- any local authority looking after a child shall make arrangements to enable him to live with
  - a parent of the child
  - a person who is not a parent but has parental responsibility
  - where the child is in care and there was a residence order in force immediately before the care order was made, the person in whose favour the residence order was made
  - a relative, friend or other person connected with him

  unless that would not be reasonably practicable or consistent with his welfare;

- where a local authority provide accommodation for a child whom they are looking after, so far as is reasonably practicable and consistent with his welfare, secure

  – the accommodation is near his home

  – siblings are accommodated together

- where a local authority provide accommodation for a child whom they are looking after and who is disabled, as far as is reasonably practicable, secure

  – the accommodation is not unsuitable for his particular needs.

(Section 23(4), (5), (6), (7) and (8))

8.3.2　The agency looking after or accommodating a child is referred to as 'the responsible authority' and they are governed by the Arrangements for Placement (General) Regulations 1991. The Regulations apply, therefore, to placements

- by a local authority of any child

- by a voluntary organisation of a child who is not looked after by a local authority

- in a registered children's home of a child who is neither looked after by a local authority nor accommodated in such a home by a voluntary organisation, by the person carrying on the home.

8.3.3　The Regulations place a duty on local authorities, voluntary organisations and registered children's homes in making arrangements to place a child to draw up and record an individual plan for the child (Regulation 3).

8.3.4　Regulation 4 and Schedules 1, 2 and 3 of the Arrangements for Placement of Children (General) Regulations 1991 list matters to be considered by the responsible authority, so far as reasonably practicable, when drawing up a plan for a child who is to be looked after or accommodated.

8.3.5　Regulation 5 lists the persons whom the responsible authority must notify in writing of the arrangements to

61

place a child; Regulation 7 details the requirements for medical examination of the child; Regulation 8, 9 and 11 relate to the establishment, retention, confidentiality and access of guardians ad litem to records; and Regulation 10 establishes the duty of responsible authorities to keep registers.

8.3.6 Regulation 13 allows for a defined series of short-term placements to be treated as a single placement for the purposes of the Regulations. The conditions in Regulation 13 are met when

- all the placements occur within a period which does not exceed one year

- no single placement is for a duration of more than four weeks, and

- the total duration of the placements does not exceed 90 days

and the placements have been "at the same place", that is to say the same carer for a family placement or at the same establishment for a residential placement.

## 8.4 Fostering

8.4.1 An earlier section of this chapter – paragraph 4.1 – dealt with private fostering. This section deals with fostering services provided by a local authority or voluntary organisation. A private or independent fostering agency may not approve foster parents.

8.4.2 Fostering is covered by The Foster Placement (Children) Regulations 1991. Except in certain emergency situations (see below, paragraph 8.4.4) a child is not to be placed unless the foster parent is an approved foster parent, and the authority and the foster parent have entered into a written agreement. A 'responsible authority' (i.e. a local authority or voluntary organisation responsible for the placement of children under the Act) may approve foster parents. Regulation 3 sets out provisions in respect of the approval of foster parents, which may be in respect of a particular child or children, or a number and age range of children, or of placements of any particular kind or in any particular circumstances.

8.4.3  The responsible authority must make arrangements for the child to be visited in the home in which he is placed, from time to time and when reasonably requested by the child or foster parent and in particular

- in the first year of the placement, within one week from its beginning and then at intervals of not more than six weeks

- subsequently, at intervals of not more than 3 months

and give such advice to the foster parent as appears to be needed (Regulation 6).

8.4.4  Regulation 8 of the Foster Placement (Children) Regulations 1991 enables a local authority to make arrangements for a voluntary organisation to discharge its duties on their behalf; Regulation 7 spells out when a placement must be terminated; Regulation 10 deals with placements outside England and Wales; and Regulation 11 relates to emergency and immediate placements by local authorities. (The powers under Regulation 11 are not available to voluntary organisations.) Under Regulation 11 a placement with an approved foster parent may be arranged for a period not exceeding 24 hours, even though the requirements for a placement agreement under Regulation 5(6) have not been satisfied. Regulation 11 also allows immediate placement with a relative or friend and requires that the relative or friend should be interviewed, the home inspected and information obtained about the other members of the household.

8.4.5  Except where arrangements have been made under Regulation 8 for a voluntary organisation to discharge the duties of a local authority on its behalf, a local authority must arrange for one of its officers to visit every child fostered in its area by or on behalf of voluntary organisations, in the following circumstances:

- within 28 days of the placement with the foster parent

- within 14 days of the receipt of representations from the voluntary organisation that there are circumstances which require a visit

- as soon as practicable but in any event within 7 days of being informed that the welfare of the child may not be being safeguarded or promoted

- at intervals of not more than six months (Regulation 15).

8.4.6 Part III of these Regulations – Regulations 12, 13 and 14 – set out requirements for records in relation to fostering.

## 8.5 Placement of Children in Care with Parents

8.5.1 As was seen above – at paragraph 6.3 – a care order will only have been made where a child is suffering or is likely to suffer significant harm and that this is attributable to the care given or likely to be given not being what it would be reasonable to expect a parent to give, or the child is beyond parental control. To place a child in care with its parents, therefore, is a complex matter. This type of placement is governed by The Placement of Children with Parents, etc, Regulations 1991.

8.5.2 However, as the Department of Health's guidance (11) points out, where it is decided that a child's best interests will be met by such a placement the local authority should look again at why the care order is still required. It may be that an arrangement could be negotiated with the parents that would enable an application for the discharge of the care order to be made. If the court discharged the order, the Regulations would not then apply. In many cases a placement under these regulations may be part of the progress towards discharge of the care order.

8.5.3 The Regulations apply when a child in care is placed for more than 24 hours with a parent, other person with parental responsibility or a person in whose favour a residence order was in force immediately before the care order was made. (This provision comes from Section

23(5)(A) which was inserted as an amendment to the Children Act 1989 by the Court and Legal Services Act 1990, Schedule 16, Paragraph 12(2).)

8.5.4   All the requirements of the Regulations must be complied with before a placement is made, except for immediate placements under Regulation 6. The Regulations require specific enquiries and assessment to be made and for a local authority to satisfy themselves that the placement is suitable. Regulation 5 requires that the Director of Social Services or his nominee(s) makes the decision on these placements because of their importance. A placement agreement must be drawn up and appropriate notifications made (Regulations 3, 4, 5, 7 and 8).

8.5.5   When circumstances require an immediate placement to be made, all the Regulations apply, but Regulation 6 provides that only the following basic checks have to be carried out before the placement:

- interviewing the parent

- inspecting the accommodation

- obtaining information about other persons living in the household

The other matters, which should be investigated in other cases before a placement, must be carried out as soon as possible.

8.5.6   As provided in the Arrangements for Placement of Children (General) Regulations (see paragraph 8.3.6 above) and the Foster Placement (Children) Regulations, so under these Regulations a defined series of short-term placements may be treated as a single placement. It should be noted that it is possible for the Placement of Children with Parents, etc., Regulations and the Foster Placement Regulations to operate in tandem, as, for example, when a child spends the week with foster parents and weekends with his parents.

8.5.7    Regulation 9 provides a framework of requirements for the social worker's task of supervision of the placement by visiting

- within one week of the beginning of the placement

- at intervals of not more than 6 weeks during the first year of the placement

- thereafter at intervals of not more than three months and also when reasonably requested by the child or the person with whom the child is placed

to give such advice and assistance as appears necessary and, so far as practicable, on each visit to see the child alone.

## 8.6    The Care of Children in Residential Homes

8.6.1    Children's Homes, under the Children Act 1989 comprise

- local authority community homes, which may be maintained, controlled or assisted community homes

- voluntary homes, carried on by non-profit-making organisations

- registered children's homes, carried on by persons or organisations which are not non-profit-making

- independent schools accommodating from 4 to 50 boarders and not approved under the Education Act 1981 for special education.

Where voluntary or private homes accommodate 4 or more children provided with personal care by reason of disablement, they come under the Registered Homes Act 1984, not the Children Act.

8.6.2    All children's homes within the meaning of the Children Act are covered by

- Arrangements for Placement of Children (General) Regulations 1991 (considered above in paragraphs 8.3.2 to 8.3.6 of this chapter)

- Children's Homes Regulations 1991

66

- Review of Children's Cases Regulations 1991 (see below)

- Representation Procedures (Children) Regulations 1991 (see below)

8.6.3 The Regulations and the Guidance provided by the Department of Health (12) are designed to provide a framework of practice for the running of children's homes which emphasises the importance of safeguarding and promoting the welfare of individual children.

8.6.4 The Children's Homes Regulations 1991 require the responsible authority to compile and maintain a statement of the purpose and functions of the home. Part II of Schedule 1 of the Regulations lists the persons to whom the statement is to be made available (Regulation 4).

8.6.5 The responsible authority must ensure that the number of staff of each children's home and their experience and qualifications are adequate to ensure that the welfare of the children accommodated there is safeguarded and promoted at all times. The staff must also have brought to their notice by the responsible authority the particulars included in the statement about the home (Regulation 5).

8.6.6 Regulation 6 requires suitable and properly equipped and furnished accommodation to be provided for each child in the home, and Regulation 7 requires the responsible authority to ensure the provision of sufficient washing, bathing and toilet facilities, adequate heating, lighting, decoration and maintenance, facilities for children to meet privately with parents and others, laundering facilities, including those to enable children to wash and iron their own clothing and access to a private pay telephone.

8.6.7 Control and discipline is governed by Regulation 8, which provides that, except as otherwise directed by the Secretary of State, only such disciplinary measures as are approved by the responsible authority may be used in a children's home and these must not include:

- any form of corporal punishment
- any deprivation of food or drink
- any restriction on visits (to or by specified persons)
- any requirement that a child wear distinctive or inappropriate clothes
- the use or withholding of medication or medical or dental treatment
- the intentional deprivation of sleep
- the imposition of fines (except by way of reparation)
- any intimate physical examination of the child.

This does not prohibit taking action in accordance with the instructions of a registered medical practitioner or any action immediately necessary to prevent injury or serious damage to property, nor the wearing of appropriate school or other organisation's uniforms, nor the imposition of restrictions on contact made under a court order.

8.6.8 Regulations 10 to 14 relate to the employment and education of older children, religious observance, food provided for children and cooking facilities, the purchase of clothes and fire precautions.

8.6.9 Part III of the Regulations relate to the administration of children's homes, including matters relating to records, notification of significant events, absence of a child without authority, the absence of the person in charge of a voluntary or registered children's home, and the visiting of homes on behalf of the responsible authority.

## 8.7 Contact between a Child who is being Looked After and Those Connected with him

8.7.1 As was noted above – at paragraph 8.2.7 – where a child is being looked after by a local authority, it has a general duty to promote contact between the child and those connected with him. This applies whether the child is accommodated by voluntary arrangement or as a result of a court order.

8.7.2 Arrangements for contact with children looked after by voluntary agreement are a matter for negotiation and agreement.

8.7.3 Where a child is in care the provisions as set out earlier – in paragraphs 6.4.5 to 6.4.10 – apply.

8.7.4 The implications for contact are among the factors which should be considered when deciding where to place a child. The Department of Health's guidance advises: "There should be a clear understanding from the outset about all the arrangements and what is expected of the parents, the responsible authority and the child's carers in connection with the arrangements." (13).

8.7.5 A provision in the Contact with Children Regulations 1991 allows for flexibility and partnership in contact arrangements, obviating the need to go back to court when all concerned agree a new arrangement. Regulation 3 provides for a local authority to depart from the terms of any order for contact under Section 34 of the Children Act when

- there is agreement between the local authority and the person in relation to whom the order is made
- the child is of sufficient understanding and agrees
- written notification of the agreement is provided within seven days to all those with a need to know.

8.7.6 When a local authority decide to vary or suspend a contact arrangement which is not governed by Section 34, with a view to affording some other person contact with a child in care, they must notify certain people with a need to know (Regulation 4).

8.7.7 Local authorities should ensure that they have clear arrangements to inform parents and others about how to pursue complaints about contact and ask for decisions to be reviewed, and these should include arrangements for parents to discuss their anxieties and dissatisfactions with senior officers if they feel they have reached an impasse with their social worker. (14).

## 8.8 Independent Visitors

8.8.1 Where it appears to a local authority in relation to any child that they are looking after that communication between the child and his parent(s), or anyone with parental responsibility for him, has been infrequent, or he has not visited or been visited or lived with any such person during the preceding twelve months, they should appoint an independent visitor, if it would be in the child's best interests (Schedule 2, Paragraph 17).

8.8.2 The person appointed shall have the duty of visiting, advising and befriending the child (Schedule 2, Paragraph 17).

8.8.3 An appointment shall not be made if the child has sufficient understanding to make an informed choice and objects to it. Similarly, the appointment can be terminated if the child objects, or where the visitor gives written notice of resignation or the authority give notice in writing that they have terminated it (Schedule 2, Paragraph 17).

8.8.4 The Definition of Independent Visitors (Children) Regulations 1991 provide that the person shall be regarded as independent

- where the person appointed is not connected with the local authority as

  - a member of the local authority or any of their committees or subcommittees

  - an officer of the local authority employed in the Social Services Department

  - a spouse of any such person

- where the child is accommodated by an organisation other than the local authority the person is not

  - a member of that organisation

  - a patron or trustee of that organisation

  - an employee - paid or not - of that organisation

  - a spouse of any such person

70

8.8.5　An independent visitor is entitled to recover from the authority reasonable expenses incurred for the purpose of his or her functions (Schedule 2, Paragraph 17).

## 8.9　Secure Accommodation

8.9.1　The Children Act 1989 makes provision, in Section 25, for the use of accommodation for the purpose of restricting liberty, and sets out the statutory framework for the restrictions of liberty. However, the Act must be read in conjunction with the Children (Secure Accommodation) Regulations 1991, which, besides detailing the provisions, also modifies and amends the effect of the Act, notably by extending the statutory safeguards governing restriction of liberty to children accommodated by health (including National Health Service Trusts) and local education authorities. Voluntary homes and registered children's homes are prohibited from providing accommodation for the purpose of restricting liberty (Regulations 7 and 18).

8.9.2　Local authorities have a duty under the Act to take reasonable steps designed to avoid the need for children within their area to be placed in secure accommodation (Schedule 2, Paragraph 7).

8.9.3　The general principles of the Act continue to apply when a placement in secure accommodation is being considered, including the duty to safeguard and promote the child's welfare, to ascertain as far as practicable the wishes and feelings of the child, his parents, other persons with parental responsibility and any other relevant person. Children provided with accommodation on a voluntary basis may be removed at any time by a person with parental responsibility for him (unless the Section 20(9) exceptions apply). This includes removal from placements in secure accommodations, whether or not the authority of the court to restrict the liberty of the child has been obtained, because the authorisation of the court is an authorisation to restrict liberty, not an order to do so. For the same reason, if at any stage the criteria for keeping a child in secure accommodation do not apply, he should be removed to alternative accommodation.

8.9.4    Section 25 of the Children Act does not apply to

- children detained under any provision of the Mental Health Act 1983

- those sentenced under Section 53 of the Children and Young Persons Act 1933

- those aged 16 or over but under 21 provided with accommodation under Section 20(5), which gives local authorities power, but not a duty, to provide such accommodation

- children subject to a child assessment order under Section 43 of the Act (see later the section of this chapter on Emergency Protection).

Different criteria apply to:

- children detained under Section 38(6) of the Police and Criminal Evidence Act 1984

- certain children remanded to local authority accommodation under Section 23 of the Children and Young Persons Act 1969, who are charged with or convicted of an offence imprisonable, in the case of a person aged 21 or over, for 14 years or more, or

- charged with or convicted of an offence of violence, or has been previously convicted of an offence of violence

(Regulations 5 and 6)

8.9.5    No child under the age of 13 years may be placed in secure accommodation in a community home without the prior approval of the Secretary of State to the placement. Such a plan should first be discussed with the Social Services Inspectorate (Regulation 4).

8.9.6    Section 25 of the Act specifies the criteria which must apply before a child may have liberty restricted. They are that

- he has a history of absconding and is likely to abscond from any other description of accommodation, and if he absconds he is likely to suffer significant harm; or

72

- if he is kept in any other description of accommodation he is likely to injure himself or other persons.

8.9.7   The maximum period beyond which a child to whom Section 25 of the Act applies may not be kept in secure accommodation without the authority of the court is an aggregate of 72 hours (whether or not consecutive) in any period of 28 consecutive days, subject to public holidays and Sundays (Regulation 10).

8.9.8   A court may authorise a child to be kept in secure accommodation up to a maximum period of three months. Where it is intended to seek the authority of the court to continue a placement in secure accommodation, the local authority looking after the child must as soon as possible notify the child's parent, any other person with parental responsibility, the independent visitor (if appointed) and any other relevant person of this intention. A court is unable to exercise its powers to authorise a period of restriction of liberty if the child is not legally represented in court, unless he has been informed of his right to apply for legal aid and has refused or failed to apply. The court must be satisfied that the relevant criteria are satisfied (Regulations 11, 14 and Sections 25(2) and 25(6)).

8.9.9   A court may from time to time authorise a child (other than a remanded child) to whom Section 25 of the Act applies to be kept in secure accommodation for a further period not exceeding 6 months at any one time (Regulation 12).

8.9.10  Section 94 of the Act provides for appeals to the High Court against decisions to authorise or refusal to authorise restrictions of liberty. When an appeal is against an authorisation a child's placement in secure accommodation may continue during consideration of the appeal, but a child must not be placed or retained in secure accommodation during consideration of an appeal against a refusal to authorise restriction of liberty.

8.9.11  In addition to the review of cases required under Section 26 of the Children Act (see below – 8.10), there are special

73

requirements in respect of the review of children in secure accommodation. Regulation 15 requires each local authority looking after a child in secure accommodation (not the local authority managing the secure unit where it is different) to ensure that his case is reviewed within one month of the start of the placement and thereafter at intervals not exceeding 3 months. Each local authority is required to appoint at least 3 people to undertake such reviews, one of whom must be independent of the authority. The persons appointed must satisfy themselves that

- the criteria for keeping the child in secure accommodation continue to apply, and

- such a placement continues to be necessary

and as far as is practicable the reviewers should ascertain and take into account the wishes and feelings of

- the child
- any parent
- any person with parental responsibility
- any other relevant person
- the child's independent visitor, if appointed
- the local authority managing the unit, if different

## 8.10 Review of Children's Cases

8.10.1 The Review of Children's Cases Regulations 1991 apply to local authorities which are looking after children and to voluntary organisations and registered children's homes which accommodate children not looked after by the local authority. The Regulations have been made by the Secretary of State for Health in the exercise of powers conferred by Section 26 of the Children Act.

8.10.2 The concept of review is a continuous process of planning and reconsiderations of the plan for the child. A specific duty is placed on the responsible authority (i.e. the local authority, voluntary organisation or person carrying on a registered children's home) to review the case of a child who is looked after or accommodated. The first review should take place no more than four weeks after the date on which the child begins to be looked after or accommodated, the second review should take place not more than three months after the first review, and subsequent reviews should take place at intervals of not more than six months (Regulations 2 and 3).

8.10.3 Each responsible authority must set out in writing their arrangements governing the manner in which cases are to be reviewed and make them known to children, parents, other persons with parental responsibility, and others considered relevant to the conduct of reviews.

8.10.4 The primary matter for consideration at the review is the plan for the welfare of the child. Schedule 2 of the Regulations provides a checklist of matters for consideration at the review, and Regulation 7(2) requires that the responsible authority, where they consider it appropriate, should involve the child and his parents in review meetings. Regulation 10 requires that a written record is drawn up and put on the child's case record, and Regulation 7(3) requires that the child, his parent, others with parental responsibility and others considered appropriate are notified of the result of the review and of decisions taken in consequence of it. Where disagreements arise in the course of the review process which cannot be resolved, the responsible authority should ensure that the child (if of sufficient understanding), parents, carers and others involved with the child are aware of the representations procedure required by the Children Act and are given advice and assistance as necessary.

8.10.5 Regulation 9 requires each responsible authority to monitor the arrangements which they have made with a view to ensuring that they comply with the Review of Children's Cases Regulations.

8.10.6 As in the other Regulations made under the Act and considered in this chapter, the review Regulations allow for a defined series of short placements to be treated as a single placement (Regulation 11).

# 9. Representations Procedure

## 9.1 The Nature of Representation

9.1.1 Responsible authorities – that is local authorities, voluntary organisations and registered children's homes – are required to have a procedure for considering representations, including complaints, about children's services. The procedure is governed by the Representations Procedure (Children) Regulations 1991. The Department of Health's guidance (15) states that the procedure should cover all representations about a local authority's actions in meeting their responsibilities to any child in need under Part III of the Act, and representations made by or on behalf of children accommodated by a voluntary organisation or registered children's home but not looked after by the local authority. This will include complaints about day care, services to support children within their family home, accommodation of a child, aftercare and decisions relating to the placement of a child or the handling of a child's case. Representations or complaints about child care matters which fall outside Part III of the Act are not covered by this procedure but by the Complaints Procedure Directions (see chapter 2, section 6).

9.1.2 The complaints procedures required for other local authority social services functions (see the next chapter of this book) are broadly compatible with the representations procedure in respect of children, and may be operated within the same structure. The main difference is that the Children Act requires the involvement of an independent person at each stage of consideration of a representation or a complaint.

9.1.3 The Department of Health's guidance (15) makes it clear that it is not intended that all problems which arise in the day to day handling of child care services should automatically be elevated into a complaint, and it will usually be possible to resolve issues satisfactorily before a complaint is made. However, attempts at problem-solving should not be used to divert an eligible person from lodging a complaint under the statutory procedure.

## 9.2 Who may make Representations?

Section 26(3) of the Act states that the procedure must provide for the consideration of any representations (including any complaint) made by

- any child who is being looked after or who is not being looked after but is in need

- a parent of his

- any person who is not a parent of his but who has parental responsibility for him

- any local authority foster parent

- such other person as the authority consider has a sufficient interest in the child's welfare to warrant his representations being considered by them.

## 9.3 The Required Procedure

9.3.1 To meet the minimum requirements of the Regulations and the Act, the responsible authority should

- designate an officer to assist in the co-ordination of all aspects of the consideration of representations

- publicise the procedure

- ensure that members of staff and independent persons are familiar with the procedure

- acknowledge all representations received by sending the complainant an explanation of the procedure and offer assistance and guidance on it or advice on where assistance and guidance may be obtained (except where the complainant is a person where it is necessary to have a preliminary stage of considering whether the person has a sufficient interest in the child's welfare to warrant his representation being considered)

- accept and record any oral representations in writing, agreeing them with the complainant

- appoint an independent person to consider the representation with the responsible authority

- consider the representation with the independent person and respond within 28 days of receipt of the representation

- give notice of their response to the complainant, and also, where different, to the person on whose behalf the representation was made and to any other persons who appear to have a sufficient interest or are otherwise involved or affected; and advise the complainant of the right to have the matter referred to a panel

- make arrangements so that where a complainant remains dissatisfied and requests (within 28 days) that his representation be reviewed, a panel is constituted to meet within 28 days of the receipt of the request; the panel of three people should include at least one independent person; the complainant, the authority and the independent person (if not the independent person on the panel) should be allowed to make oral or written submissions to the panel; and the complainant may be accompanied at a panel meeting by another person of his choice who may speak on his behalf.

- ensure that the panel's recommendation is recorded in writing within 24 hours of the completion of their deliberations and sent formally to the responsible authority, to the complainant, to the first stage independent person and to anyone else with a sufficient interest in the case

- consider together with the independent person appointed to the panel, what actions to take having due regard to the findings of those considering the representation

- notify the authority's decision in the matter and their reasons for it and any action they have taken or propose to take, to the person making the representation, the child (if of sufficient understanding) and such other persons as appear to be likely to be affected

- keep a record of all representations and the outcome of each case

- provide an annual report of the operation of the procedure.

## 9.4 Links with Other Procedures

9.4.1 The procedure required by these Regulations is not an appeal procedure; separate procedures exist for appeals against the usual fostering limit exemption, and appeals against court orders are to the court.

9.4.2 The second stage panel does not affect an individual's right to make a complaint to the Local Commissioner (or ombudsman) about local authority maladministration, as the panel is not a decision-making body. Similarly, it does not affect an individual's or organisation's right to approach a local councillor.

9.4.3 The Department of Health's guidance (15) advises that, if a representation is made which involves more than one local authority, it should be considered by the local authority which is looking after the child. If the child is not being looked after but provided with other services the local authority in whose area the child normally lives should consider the complaint. It also advises that arrangements should provide for separating out representations appropriate to another procedure or for joint action with other procedures including those within health authorities and other agencies contributing to child care services.

9.4.4 The handling of a complaint may be concurrent with action under disciplinary procedures, action in respect of child protection or a police investigation.

# 10. Protection of Children

## 10.1 General Duty of Local Authorities

10.1.1 Schedule 2, Paragraph 4 of the Children Act states:

"Every local authority shall take reasonable steps, through the provision of services under Part III of this Act, to prevent children within their area suffering ill-treatment or neglect."

Thus, in a general way, the authority's services are directed at child protection, and as noted earlier – at paragraph 2.6 of this chapter – Section 27 of the Act lays a duty on certain other authorities to co-operate with the social services department when it is exercising its general duty of safeguarding and promoting the welfare of children.

10.1.2 The Children Act, however, makes no reference to the systems for child protection registers (or 'at risk registers' or 'the abuse register' as they are variously known) or for Area Child Protection Committees or for Child Protection Conferences which have been in existence for some time. These systems are fundamental to the structure of child protection, but are the creation not of statute but of a Department of Health and Social Security (as it then was) Circular, 'Working Together' (1988).

This has now been radically revised into a new set of guidance entitled "Working Together under the Children Act 1989" (HMSO 1991). The Area Child Protection Committee is the forum for developing, monitoring and reviewing child protection policies. Its main functions, as set out in 'Working Together' are

- to establish, maintain and review local inter-agency guidelines on procedures to be followed in individual cases

- to monitor the implementations of legal procedures

- to identify significant issues arising from the handling of cases and reports from inquiries

- to scrutinise arrangements to provide treatment, expert advice and inter-agency liaison and make recommendations to the responsible agencies
- to scrutinise progress on work to prevent child abuse and make recommendations to the responsible agencies
- to scrutinise work related to inter-agency training and make recommendations to the responsible agencies
- to conduct case reviews as required by the Guide
- to publish an annual report about local child protection matters.

The Child Protection Conference or Case Conference is the basic instrument of a local child protection system, and is the forum for multi-disciplinary consideration of a child thought to be 'at risk'. The discussions should be confidential, but this raises legal issues about parental involvement and access to records of case conferences. The case conference will look at the child in question and recommend at the initial conference whether the child's name should be placed on the child protection register. The register "is essentially a management tool that records the fact that a child has been or is suspected of being abused or is believed to be at risk of being abused .... It is not a 'legal' document, it has no statutory force and of itself offers no 'real' protection, in that the mere act of placing a child's name on the protection register does not give any agency the legal grounds to take any action in relation to that child." (16) It is to Part V of the Children Act 1989 that one must turn for the legal structure for the protection of children.

## 10.2 The Duty to Investigate

10.2.1 Where a local authority

- have reasonable cause to suspect that a child who lives, or is found, in their area is suffering, or is likely to suffer significant harm; or

- are informed that a child who lives or is found in their area is the subject of an emergency protection order or is in police protection;

they must make, or cause to be made (e.g. by the NSPCC) such enquiries as they consider necessary to enable them to decide whether they should take any action to safeguard or promote the child's welfare (Section 47(1)).

10.2.2 Similarly, the local authority is under a duty to investigate for the same purpose where they have themselves obtained an emergency protection order (Section 47(2)).

10.2.3 As noted earlier in this chapter, the local authority also have a duty to investigate where a court in family proceedings directs them to investigate a child's circumstances or where a local education authority notify them that a child is persistently failing to comply with directions given under an education supervision order.

10.2.4 Where enquiries are being made under Section 47(1) – see above – the local authority must take such steps as are reasonably practicable to obtain access to the child in question or to ensure that access to him is obtained on their behalf, with a view to enabling them to determine what action, if any, to take, unless they are satisfied that they already have sufficient information (Section 47(4)).

10.2.5 Where as a result of the enquiries, it appears to the authority that there are matters concerned with the child's education which should be investigated, they must consult the relevant education authority (Section 47(5)).

10.2.6 Where, in the course of making enquiries access to the child, or information as to his whereabouts, is denied, the local authority must apply for an emergency protection order, a child assessment order, a care order or a supervision order, unless they are satisfied that the child's welfare can be satisfactorily safeguarded without an application (Section 47(6)).

10.2.7 If, as a result of their enquiries, the authority decide not to apply for any of the above orders, they must consider whether it would be appropriate to review the case at a later date, and if so set a date for the review to begin (Section 47(7)).

10.2.8 Unless unreasonable to do so, it is the duty of the following to assist the local authority in the conduct of their enquiries, in particular by providing relevant information and advice,

- any local authority
- any local education authority
- any local housing authority
- any health authority
- any person authorised by the Secretary of State.

## 10.3 Child Assessment Orders

10.3.1 The child assessment order deals with the specific issue of examination or assessment of a child when there is non-co-operation by the parents and lack of evidence of the need for a different type of order or other action. It is not for use in emergencies. However, the court may treat an application for a child assessment order as an application for an emergency protection order. This is the one exception under Part V of the Act, to the general rule that the court must either make or refuse to make the order applied for and cannot make any other kind of order. This is because proceedings under Part V are not 'family proceedings' for the purpose of the Act, unlike other proceedings considered earlier in this Chapter, where the courts have flexibility about which orders to make (Section 43(3) and (4)).

10.3.2 Only a local authority or authorised person may apply for a child assessment order, and the court may make the order if satisfied that

- the applicant has reasonable cause to suspect that the child is suffering, or is likely to suffer, significant harm;

- an assessment of the state of the child's health or development, or the way in which he has been treated, is required to enable the applicant to determine whether or not the child is suffering, or is likely to suffer, significant harm; and

- it is unlikely that such an assessment will be made, or be satisfactory, in the absence of an order (Section 43(1)).

10.3.3 The order must specify the date on which the assessment is to begin and has effect for such period as the order specifies, not exceeding 7 days (Section 43(5)).

10.3.4 Under the order, it is the duty of any person who is in a position to produce the child

- to produce him to persons named in the order

- to comply with directions in the order (Section 43(6)).

10.3.5 The order authorises the person carrying out the assessment to do so in accordance with the terms of the order, but a child of sufficient understanding to make an informed decision may refuse a medical, psychiatric or other assessment. The child may only be kept away from home in accordance with directions in the order, if it is necessary and for such period as specified in the order. Where a child is kept away from home, directions regarding contact must be included in the order (Section 43(7), (8), (9) and (10)).

10.3.6 The applicant must take reasonable steps to ensure that notice of the application is given to

- the child's parents

- any other person with parental responsibility

- any other person caring for the child

- any person in whose favour a contact order is in force

- any person entitled to have contact with a child in care

- the child.

10.3.7 The Department of Health's guidance suggests that a child assessment order will usually be most appropriate where the harm to the child is long-term and cumulative rather than sudden and severe and recommend that it should be used sparingly. It states: "Any proposal to apply for a child assessment order and the arrangements to be discussed with the court for the assessment should be considered at a case conference convened under local child protection procedures". (17)

10.3.8 Rules of court provide for the circumstances in which and by whom an application to vary or discharge a child assessment order may be made. There is a right of appeal against the making or refusal to make an order, and a court may prevent a further application without leave or refuse to allow a further application within six months without leave (Section 91(14) and (15)).

10.3.9 Where there is deliberate refusal to comply with a child assessment order, there is likely to be added concern for the child's welfare and would probably be sufficient to satisfy the conditions for an emergency protection order.

## 10.4 Emergency Protection Orders

10.4.1 The emergency protection order is designed to enable a child in a genuine emergency to be removed or to be kept where he is, if this is necessary to provide short-term protection. It may be that an abuser could be removed from a family home under private law remedies, by using exclusion orders under the Domestic Violence and Matrimonial Proceedings Act 1976 or the Domestic Proceedings and Magistrates' Court Act 1978. There is no such power in public law, but there is provision under the Children Act for a local authority to assist a person to obtain alternative accommodation, including cash assistance, where a child is suffering or likely to suffer ill-treatment at the hands of a person living on the premises (Schedule 2, Paragraph 5).

10.4.2 Any person may apply for a emergency protection order. In practice most applications are likely to be made by local authorities or authorised persons (i.e. the NSPCC). However, rules of court require the applicant to notify the local authority, whose duty to investigate then applies. There is also provision, when an order has been made on the application of some individual or authorised person for the local authority to take over the order, under the Emergency Protection Orders (Transfer of Responsibilities) Regulations 1991.

10.4.3 The court may make an order if it is satisfied that

- there is reasonable cause to believe that the child is likely to suffer significant harm if

  - he is not removed to accommodation provided by or on behalf of the applicant; or

  - he does not remain in the place where he is being accommodated;

- in the case of an application made by a local authority, enquiries are being made under Section 47 and those enquiries are being frustrated by access to the child being unreasonably refused and the applicant has reasonable cause to believe that access to the child is required as a matter of urgency; or

- in the case of an application by an authorised person, the applicant has reasonable cause to suspect that a child is suffering, or is likely to suffer, significant harm, and is making enquiries into the child's welfare and those enquiries are being frustrated by access to the child being unreasonably refused and the applicant has reasonable cause to believe that access is required as a matter of urgency (Section 44(1)).

10.4.4 As with all orders under the Children Act, the court will not automatically make an emergency protection order even where the above conditions apply, as it must still consider the welfare principle and the presumption of no order.

10.4.5 Because of the emergency nature of the applications, it is likely that many applications will be heard *ex parte* (i.e. without others being given notice of the hearing and being present). Rules of court require the applicant to serve a copy of the application and the order on the parties to the proceedings within 48 hours. Explanatory notes on the back of the order explain what will happen to the child and what the parents can do next.

10.4.6 The effects of an emergency protection order are that it

- directs any person who is in a position to do so to comply with any request to produce the child to the applicant

- authorises the removal or prevention of removal of the child

- gives the applicant parental responsibility for the child (Section 44(4)).

10.4.7 However, the applicant can only exercise the power to remove or detain the child in order to safeguard the welfare of the child, so if the child is found to be safe it should not be used. Similarly, the exercise of parental responsibility should only be such as is reasonably required to safeguard and promote the welfare of the child, having regard to the duration of the order (Section 44(5) and (10)).

10.4.8 The court may give such direction (if any) as it considers appropriate with respect to contact with the child and the medical, psychiatric or other assessment of the child. If the child is of sufficient understanding to make an informed decision, he may refuse to submit to such examination or assessment. Subject to any direction of the court the applicant must allow reasonable contact with

- his parents

- any person with parental responsibility

- any person with whom he was living immediately before the making of the order

- any person with a contact order in force
- if in care, any person allowed contact with the child
- any person acting on behalf of any of the above (Section 44(6), (7) and (13)).

10.4.9 An emergency protection order has effect for such period as is specified, not exceeding eight days. The court may grant an extension, once only, for a period not exceeding seven days. Rules of court require an application for an extension to be made on notice at a full *inter-partes* hearing (Section 45(1), (4), (5) and (6)).

10.4.10 If the applicant for an emergency protection order does not know the whereabouts of a child, but that information seems to be available to another person, the court may order that person to disclose the information when requested by the applicant. The order may also authorise the applicant to enter specified premises and search for the child. The Department of Health guidance (18) recommends that applicants ask for this authority as a matter of course to avoid unnecessary return to court (Section 48(1) and (3)).

10.4.11 Where a court is satisfied that there is reasonable cause to believe that there may be another child on such premises with respect to whom an emergency protection order ought to be made, it may make an order authorising the applicant to search for that other child. Where such a second child is found, the order authorising the search shall have effect as if it were an emergency protection order. The applicant must notify the court of this (Section 48(4), (5) and (6)).

10.4.12 It is a criminal offence intentionally to obstruct an authorised person exercising his powers to enter and search premises for the child. If this happens or is likely to happen, the court may issue a warrant authorising any constable to assist the authorised person in entering and searching the specified premises. In granting such a warrant the court may direct that the constable be

88

accompanied by a registered medical practitioner, nurse or health visitor if he so chooses (Section 48(7), (9) and (11)).

10.4.13 In extreme emergencies the police have powers under the Police and Criminal Evidence Act 1984, Section 17(1)(e), to enter and search premises without a warrant for the purpose of saving life and limb, and may, under Section 25(3)(e) of that Act, arrest without a warrant where the constable has reasonable grounds for believing that arrest is necessary to protect a child from the relevant person.

10.4.14 Any of the following may apply to the court for an emergency protection order to be discharged

- the child

- his parent(s)

- any other person with parental responsibility

- any person with whom he was living immediately before the making of the order.

No application for discharge can be heard before the expiry of 72 hours from the making of the order, and cannot be made if the person was given notice and was present at the hearing at which the order was made; nor can there be an application for the discharge of an order that has been extended (Section 45(8), (9) and (11)).

10.4.15 There is no right of appeal against the making, refusal to make, extension of or refusal to extend, the discharge of or refusal to discharge an emergency protection order or the giving of or refusal to give directions in the order. It is possible, however, to apply for directions to be varied (Section 45(10) and 44(9)).

## 10.5 Police Protection

10.5.1 Where a constable has reasonable cause to believe that a child would otherwise be likely to suffer significant harm he may remove the child to suitable accommodation and keep him there or take such steps as are reasonable to ensure the child's removal from a hospital, or other place in which he is then accommodated, is prevented. This is known as police protection. The constable must then ensure that the case is inquired into by a 'designated officer' (i.e. designated for this purpose by the Chief Constable), who must release the child unless he believes there is still reasonable cause for believing that the child would be likely to suffer significant harm if released (Section 46(1), (2), (3) and (5)).

10.5.2 No child may be kept in police protection for more than 72 hours (Section 46(6)).

10.5.3 The constable, as soon as reasonably practicable after taking the child into police protection, must

- inform the local authority

- inform the child (if he appears capable of under-standing) of the steps taken, the reasons for them and of further steps that may be taken

- discover the wishes and feelings of the child as far as reasonably practicable

- move the child to accommodation provided by the local authority or to a refuge

- inform the parents, other persons with parental res-ponsibility and any person with whom the child was living, as far as is reasonably practicable (Section 46(3)).

10.5.4 The designated officer *must*

- allow the parents, other persons with parental responsibility, any person with whom the child was living, any person with a contact order or right of contact with a child in care, or any person acting of behalf of these persons, to have such contact as is reasonable and in the child's best interests

- do what is reasonable in all the circumstances to promote the child's welfare, although the police do not acquire parental responsibility

90

and the designated officer *may*

- apply on behalf of the local authority for an emergency protection order, whether or not the authority know of the application or agree with it

but the police cannot apply for an extension to an order (Section 46(7), (8), (9) and (10)).

## 10.6 Recovery Orders

10.6.1 It is an offence if a person knowingly and without lawful authority or reasonable excuse takes or keeps a child who is in care, or the subject of an emergency protection order or in police protection from the responsible person, or induces, assists or incites such a child to run away or stay away from the responsible person (Section 49).

10.6.2 Where a court has reason to believe that such a child has been unlawfully taken or kept away from the responsible person, or has run away or is staying away or is missing, it may make a 'recovery order' (Section 50(1) and (2)).

10.6.3 The effects of a recovery order are

- to direct any person who is in a position to do so to produce the child on request to any authorised person

- to allow a person authorised by the court to remove the child

- to require any person who has information as to the child's whereabouts to disclose it to a constable or officer of the court, if requested

- to authorise a constable to enter any premises specified in the order and search for the child, using reasonable force if necessary.

It is an offence intentionally to obstruct an authorised person exercising the power to remove the child (Section 50(3) and (9)).

10.6.4 Applications for recovery orders can be made only by those with parental responsibility for the child by virtue of a care order or emergency protection order, or the designated officer where the child is in police protection. An authorised person should produce some duly authenticated document showing that he is authorised and that this is related to the recovery order (Section 50(4) and (8)).

## 10.7 Refuges for Children at Risk

10.7.1 Section 51 of the Children Act 1989 provides a way by which *bona fide* organisations which provide refuges for runaway youngsters can be exempted from prosecution for assisting them to run away or stay away or for harbouring them or for child abduction.

This is provided for by means of a power given to the Secretary of State to issue certificates to

- voluntary homes
- registered homes, or
- foster parents approved by local authorities or voluntary organisations,

which have the effect of certain provisions not applying to them.

10.7.2 Applications under this provision should be made on the prescribed form to Community Services Division (CS2C) Department of Health, Room 216, Wellington House, 133-155 Waterloo Road, London, SE1 8UG.

10.7.3 Provisions as to the issue and withdrawal of certificates and requirements while a certificate is in force are contained in the Refuges for Children at Risk (Children's Homes and Foster Placements) Regulations 1991.

10.7.4 Under the regulations the police have to be informed of every admission within 24 hours, with a view to the parent or other specified person being notified that the child is in a refuge and provided with a telephone contact number, but not the address (Regulation 3).

# 11. Adoption

## 11.1 Background to Adoption Legislation

11.1.1 Adoption is the ultimate long-term placement for children for whom it is clear they will never be able to return to their parents or other members of their family, and for whom long-term residential care is inappropriate.

11.1.2 The key legislation governing adoption has for many years been the Adoption Act 1958. This legislation addressed the situation where there were significant numbers of babies and young children, often illegitimate, available for adoption by childless couples. But over the years the position has changed a great deal, with attitudes, social behaviour, family patterns, international travel and new insights all affecting adoption law and practice. The Adoption Act 1960 addressed issues of legitimacy, the Adoption Act 1964 made provisions in respect of documents in Northern Ireland and Scotland, the Adoption Act 1968 dealt with the recognition of adoptions and adoption proceedings taking place overseas, and the Children Act 1975 was passed following the Houghton Committee's (19) consideration of law, policy and procedure on the adoption of children. The Children Act 1975 was subject to piecemeal implementation. The Adoption Act 1976 consolidated the law on adoption as found in the legislation mentioned above, but did not itself come into force until 1 January 1988. The major changes introduced by the Children Act 1989 have had significant impact on adoption law, which is now the subject of a review set in motion by the government.

11.1.3 This section of this chapter seeks, therefore, to set out the current position in broad terms, as it is an area of law of some complexity and likely to be overhauled in the future.

## 11.2 Adoption Services

11.2.1 Since 1982 it has been a criminal offence for private individuals to arrange adoption placements, unless the proposed adopter is a relative as defined by Section 72(1) of the Adoption Act 1976; otherwise only adoption agencies may do so.

11.2.2 The Adoption Act 1976 imposes on each local authority a duty to ensure the provision of a comprehensive adoption service, either by acting itself as an adoption agency or by means of a voluntary adoption agency which has been approved by the Secretary of State, in accordance with the Act (Adoption Act 1976, Section 1).

11.2.3 The service should meet the needs in relation to adoption of children who have or may be adopted, of parents and guardians of such children, and of persons who have adopted or may adopt. This includes making arrangements for the assessment of children and prospective adopters, placing children for adoption and providing counselling for persons with problems in relation to adoption (Adoption Act 1976, Section 1(1) and (2)).

11.2.4 The detailed duties of adoption agencies are specified by the Adoption Agencies Regulations 1983.

## 11.3 Duties of Adoption Agencies

11.3.1 The Adoption Agencies Regulations set out the areas which must be investigated and reported upon in respect of a child being considered for adoption and the prospective adopters. In practice most agencies use the forms provided by the British Agencies for Adoption and Fostering (BAAF), which have been designed to comply with the Adoption Agencies Regulations 1983. Form E relates to the child needing a family placement and Form F relates to the prospective substitute parent(s).

11.3.2 The Regulations require every adoption agency to establish an Adoption Panel, and in the case of a local authority this must not be a sub-committee of the Social Services Committee. The panel should comprise not more than ten members and not less than seven, with a quorum of five. At least two of the panel members must be independent of the agency, two must be social workers employed by the agency, at least one must represent the

94

management committee of the agency or the social services committee, and there must be a medical advisor. The chairperson should preferably be a qualified social worker.

11.3.3 The Adoption Panel must consider and make recommendations as follows:

- whether adoption is in the best interests of the child. Having considered that the child is suitable for adoption, the panel should consider whether or not the child should be freed for adoption;

- whether a prospective adopter is suitable to be an adoptive parent;

- whether a prospective adopter would be a suitable adoptive parent for a particular child.

The regulations make it clear that the approval and matching process need not take place at the same meeting.

11.3.4 The agency must await the panel's recommendations before making a decision, but it would be unusual not to follow it. If it decides to place a child with a particular adopter it must notify the adopter, the child, the child's parents and the health, education and local authorities. It must also ensure that the child is visited within one week of being placed and as often as necessary thereafter and reports of the visits maintained. An application for an adoption order must be made to the court within three months of the placement, otherwise the placement must be reviewed.

11.3.5 Where an application is made to adopt a child placed by an agency, the agency has a duty to prepare a report for the court hearing the application. The required contents of the report are specified in Schedule 2 of the Adoption Rules 1984.

## 11.4 Who may Adopt and be Adopted

11.4.1 Applications to adopt may be made

- jointly by married couples, both of whom are aged twenty-one or over

- jointly by a married couple, where one is aged at least twenty-one and the other is the mother or father of the child and is aged at least eighteen

- by a single applicant aged at least twenty-one

- by a sole applicant who is married, but the court must be satisfied that

  - the spouse cannot be found

  - the spouses have separated and are living apart and the separation is likely to be permanent; or

  - the spouse is incapable of making an application by reason of ill-health.

- by a sole applicant who is the mother or father of the child, but the court must be satisfied that

  - the other natural parent is dead or cannot be found; or

  - there is some other reason justifying the exclusion of the other natural parent.

(Section 14(1), Adoption Act 1976 as amended by Children Act 1989, Schedule 10, Paragraph 4; and Section 15(1), Adoption Act 1976)

11.4.2　A sole adopter must be domiciled in the United Kingdom, and in the case of a joint application at least one of the applicants must be so domiciled. (Adoption Act 1976, Section 14(1) and (2) and 15(1) and (2)).

11.4.3　An unmarried person under the age of eighteen years is eligible to be adopted (Adoption Act 1976, Section 72(1)).

11.4.4　An order cannot be made unless the child has had his home with the applicant for at least 13 weeks. Since the parent cannot give agreement until the child is at least 6 weeks old, the child must therefore be at least 19 weeks old.

## 11.5 Adoption Proceedings

11.5.1 Adoption proceedings are 'family proceedings' as defined by the Children Act 1989. Therefore, a Section 8 order may be made at any time during them. As in other family proceedings, if the court considers that it may be appropriate to make a care or supervision order, it may direct the local authority to investigate the child's circumstances.

11.5.2 An adoption order cannot be made unless the parent(s) or guardian(s) of the child give agreement to the order, except where parental agreement has been dispensed with or an order 'freeing' the child for adoption has been made. Agreement must be given freely and unconditionally, and with full understanding of what is involved. It may be withdrawn at any time up to the making of the order, subject to the court's power to dispense with agreement (Adoption Act 1976, Section 16(1)).

11.5.3 It is possible for the agreement to the making of the order to be dispensed with on the following grounds

- the parent(s) or guardian(s) cannot be found or is incapable of giving agreement
- the parent or guardian is withholding agreement unreasonably
- the parent or guardian has persistently failed without reasonable cause to discharge the obligations of a parent or guardian of the child
- the parent or guardian has abandoned or neglected the child
- the parent or guardian has seriously ill-treated the child

(Adoption Act 1976, Section 16(2)).

11.5.4 Once an application to adopt has been made, to which the parents have agreed, the parents cannot remove the child against the wishes of the applicant except by leave of court. When a freeing application has been made by an agency, a similar restriction applies except that it also applies to parents who have not agreed. Similarly, an adoption agency cannot remove a child from the prospective adopters once an application to adopt has been made (Adoption Act 1976, Section 27(1) and (2) and Section 30(2)).

11.5.5 When an application is made for an adoption order, or notice of the intention to apply has been given to the local authority, by a person with whom the child has had his home for five years, no person is entitled to remove the child against the will of the applicant except by leave of the court (Adoption Act 1976, Section 28).

11.5.6 If it appears that the parents or guardian of the child are willing to agree to the adoption, the court, as soon as possible after the application, must appoint a reporting officer. The reporting officer's function is to verify that the requirements concerning agreement are satisfied, and to report to the court, drawing its attention to any matters which may be of assistance in considering the application (Adoption Rules 1984, Rule 17).

11.5.7 If it appears that the parents or guardian are unwilling to give agreement or there are other special circumstances, the court must, as soon as possible, appoint a guardian ad litem. The guardian ad litem's role is to safeguard the interests of the child by investigating and reporting on any relevant matters, particularly those covered in the adoption agency's report or the statement of facts to be relied upon for dispensing with agreement. The guardian ad litem should also advise on whether the child should attend the hearing, and must fulfil any other duty requested by the court (Adoption Rules 1984, Rule 18).

11.5.8 The hearing is held in private. The child and the applicants must usually attend, and any person who is a respondent to the application may attend. The court may require the attendance of any other person it considers necessary.

11.5.9 An adoption order gives parental responsibility for a child to the adopters and extinguishes the parental responsibility of others. An adopted child is treated as if it were the legitimate child of the adoptive parents. For the purposes of the law against incest and the prohibited degrees of marriage, however, the child is regarded as a member of its natural family. An adoption order is irrevocable, except where the child has been adopted by a single parent who subsequently marries the other parent so that the child is legitimated by operation of law (Adoption Act 1976, Section 12 (as amended by Children Act 1989, Schedule 10), Sections 39, 47, 48, 49 and 52).

11.5.10 Applicants who are refused an order are debarred from making a further application for adoption unless the court making the refusal directs otherwise or there has been a change of circumstances making it reasonable to proceed (Adoption Act 1976, Section 24(1)).

## 11.6 Freeing for Adoption

11.6.1 The above proceedings relate essentially to a specific adoption application by particular applicants. There is also the procedure whereby an adoption agency may apply to a court for an order freeing a child for adoption, more generally. This enables the agency to make the decision for a child to be placed with applicants, who may already be selected or may be selected later, without consulting the natural parents.

11.6.2 At least one of the child's parents must agree to the application unless application is also made for the agreement of both parents to be dispensed with. If the child is already in the care of the agency then an application for the agreement of both parents to be dispensed with can be made. If the child is not already in the care of the agency, one parent must agree to the application. The court may not dispense with the agreement of the parents unless the child is actually placed with adopters or it is satisfied that he is likely to be (Adoption Act 1976, Section 18(1), (2) and (3)).

11.6.3　Before making a freeing order, the court must be satisfied that each parent has been asked if he or she wishes to make a declaration that he or she prefers not to be involved in further questions about the child's adoption. If a declaration is made, it must be recorded by the court, and the former parents will have no further involvement in the child's adoption. If no declaration is made, the agency must inform the parents within fourteen days of the first anniversary of the freeing order if an adoption order has been made or the child placed for adoption (Adoption Act 1976 Section 18(6) and Section (19)).

11.6.4　An application to revoke a freeing order may be made by a parent or guardian at any time after twelve months since the making of the order, provided that the child has not been adopted or placed for adoption. Once an application for revocation has been made, the agency cannot place the child for adoption without leave of the court (Adoption Act 1976, Section 20(1) and (2)).

## 11.7 Access to Birth Records and Birth Parents

11.7.1　Every adoption must be recorded in the Adopted Children Register, maintained by the Registrar General. On reaching the age of eighteen, an adopted person has the right to a copy of his or her original birth certificate. Where the adoption order was made before 12 November 1975, the certificate will only be released after counselling; those adopted after 12 November 1975 can choose whether or not to see a counsellor (Adoption Act 1976, Sections 50 and 51).

11.7.2　The Children Act 1989 has amended the Adoption Act 1976 to permit the counselling to be obtained either anywhere within the United Kingdom or from a body outside the United Kingdom which has notified the Registrar General that it is willing to provide counselling and satisfies the Registrar that it is suitable to do so (Schedule 10, Paragraph 20).

11.7.3　The Children Act 1989 also requires the Registrar General to set up an Adoption Contact Register to enable adopted people to contact their birth parents and other relatives. The register is in two parts: Part I – Adopted Persons, and Part II – Relatives. The Registrar General, on payment of the prescribed fee, shall enter in Part I the name and address of any adopted person aged 18 or over who gives notice that he wishes to contact any relative of his. Similarly, a relative – meaning any person (other than an adoptive relative) who is related to the adopted person by blood (including half-blood) or marriage – may be reg-istered in Part II. The Registrar General must then transmit to an adopted person whose name is entered in Part I the name and address of any relative for whom there is an entry in Part II. Entry on the register can be cancelled by notice to the Registrar General and the address may be any address at or through which the person concerned may be contacted, not necessarily where the person is living (Schedule 10, Paragraph 21).

11.7.4 Leaflets about the Adoption Contact Register and about Access to Birth Records have been produced by the Department of Health and are reproduced in Volume 9 of the Children Act 1989 Guidance and Regulations, entitled 'Adoption Issues'.

## References

1. Department of Health (1991) "The Children Act Guidance and Regulations" HMSO, London, Volume 2, Paragraph 1.6.

2. Department of Health (1991) "The Children Act Guidance and Regulations" HMSO, London, Volume 2, Paragraphs 4.9, 4.10 and 4.13.

3. Department of Health (1991) "The Children Act Guidance and Regulations" HMSO, London, Volume 2, Paragraph 7.33.

4. Department of Health (1991) "The Children Act Guidance and Regulations" HMSO, London, Volume 4.

5. Department of Health (1991) "The Children Act Guidance and Regulations" IIMSO, London, Volume 1, Paragraphs 1.17 and 1.18.

6.  Department of Health (1991) "The Children Act Guidance and Regulations" HMSO, London, Volume 1, Paragraphs 3.1, 3.2, 3.3, 3.4 and 3.5.

7.  Department of Health (1991) "The Children Act Guidance and Regulations" HMSO, London, Volume 1, Paragraph 3.68.

8.  Department of Health (1991) "The Children Act Guidance and Regulations" HMSO, London, Volume 1, Paragraph 3.76.

9.  Department of Health (1991) "The Children Act Guidance and Regulations" HMSO, London, Volume 1, Paragraph 3.58.

10. Department of Health (1991) "The Children Act Guidance and Regulations" HMSO, London, Volume 3 and 4, Paragraph 2.10.

11. Department of Health (1991) "The Children Act Guidance and Regulations" HMSO, London, Volume 3 and 4, Paragraph 5.2.

12. Department of Health (1991) "The Children Act Guidance and Regulations" HMSO, London, Volume 4.

13. Department of Health (1991) "The Children Act Guidance and Regulations" HMSO, London, Volume 4, Paragraph 4.14.

14. Department of Health (1991) "The Children Act Guidance and Regulations" HMSO, London, Volume 4, Paragraphs 4.36 and 4.37.

15. Department of Health (1991) "The Children Act Guidance and Regulations" HMSO, London, Volume 4.

16. Brayne, H. and Martin, G. (1990) "Law for Social Workers", Blackstone Press, London.

17. Department of Health (1991) "The Children Act 1989 Guidance and Regulations" HMSO, London, Volume 1, Paragraphs 4.9 and 4.23.

18. Department of Health (1991) "The Children Act 1989 Guidance and Regulations" HMSO, London, Volume 1, Paragraphs 4.50 and 4.52.

19. Houghton Committee (1972) "Report of the Departmental Committee on the Adoption of Children", HMSO, London, Cmnd 5107.

# Chapter Two
# The Care of Adults in the Community

## Introduction

In 1986 the Secretary of State for Social Services asked Sir Roy Griffiths to undertake an overview of community care policy. The outcome was what has come to be called the Griffiths Report 'Community Care: Agenda for Action' (1), published in February 1988. There followed, in 1989, a White Paper 'Caring for People: Community Care in the Next Decade and Beyond' (2), which was translated into legislation, by finding expression in the National Health Service and Community Care Act 1990.

There had already been, in 1983, a review of the management of the health service, and in 1985 Lady Wagner was appointed "to review the role of residential care". This led to the report 'Residential Care: A Positive Choice' (3) in 1988. The Audit Commission also reported in December 1986 on 'Making a Reality of Community Care'. These various reviews and reports played into creating what the Government now calls the policy framework for community care in the next decade and beyond.

As far as the law is concerned, however, it has developed in a higgledy-piggledy way, producing overlaps between legislation relating to old people, people with physical disabilities, people with mental illnesses and learning difficulties, and children with disabilities.

The Children Act 1989 has produced a largely coherent and comprehensive code for the law relating to all children. (The Children Act specifically seeks to integrate provision for disabled children into the overall framework, but Volume 6 of the Department of Health's Guidance draws together those aspects which relate to children with disabilities.) It is also possible to set out a reasonably discrete area of law relating to people with mental illnesses or disabilities, and this is the focus of Chapter 3. The developing community care legislation is essentially in respect of adults, and primarily in respect of adults who are old or have physical disabilities. They are the focus of this chapter on the care of adults in the community.

It is a developing area, with policy as well as legislation – some yet to be implemented – shaping what services and practices are taking place. Consequently the law on the community care of adults has very much to be read in the context of policy development and the partial or delayed implementation of legislation.

## 1. Community Care Planning

1.1 Section 46 of the National Health Service and Community Care Act 1990 requires each local authority to

- prepare and publish a plan for the provision of community care services in their area

- keep the plan prepared by them and any further plans under review

- prepare and publish modifications to the plan, or if the case requires, a new plan, at such intervals as the Secretary of State may direct.

The Secretary of State has directed that the first plans must be produced by 1 April 1992.

1.2 In preparing their plans, local authorities must consult

- any District Health Authority whose district lies within the area of the local authority

- any Family Health Services Authority whose locality lies within the area of the local authority

- such local housing authority whose area is within the area of the local authority, if the local authority is not itself a local housing authority

- such voluntary organisations as appear to the authority to represent the interests of persons who use or are likely to use any community care services within the area or the interests of private carers who, within the area, provide care to persons for whom the local authority have a power or duty to provide a service

- such voluntary housing agencies and other bodies as appear to the local authority to provide housing or community care services in their area

- such other persons as the Secretary of State may direct (National Health Service and Community Care Act 1990, Section 46(2))

1.3 Community Care services means services which a local authority may provide or arrange to be provided under any of the following provisions

- Part III of the National Assistance Act 1948

- Section 45 of the Health Services and Public Health Act 1968

- Section 21 of and Schedule 8 to the National Health Service Act 1977

- Section 117 of the Mental Health Act 1983.

However, provisions under this list of legislation does not comprise the whole of the community care services, as later sections of this chapter will show, and many local authorities' community care plans are likely to go wider and integrate their other duties to adults in the community (National Health Service and Community Care Act 1990, Section 46(3)).

1.4 The Department of Health's Policy Guidance (4) advises Social Services Departments and NHS authorities on what is expected of them to meet national policy objectives in planning community care, and sets out the Government's policy framework as follows:

"It aims to enable people to live an independent and dignified life at home, or elsewhere within the community, for as long as they are able and wish to do."

The key objectives are:

- to promote the development of domiciliary, day and respite services to enable people to live in their own homes wherever feasible and sensible

- to ensure that service providers make practical support for carers a high priority

- to make proper assessment of need and good care management the cornerstone of high quality care

- to promote the development of a flourishing independent sector alongside good quality public services

105

- to clarify the responsibilities of agencies and so make it easier to hold them to account for their performance
- to secure better value for tax payers' money by introducing a new funding structure for social care.

Therefore, it states that in their plans social services departments should identify

- **Assessment**
  - the care needs of the local population, taking into account such factors as age distribution, problems associated with living in inner city areas or rural areas, special needs of ethnic minority communities, the number of homeless or transient people likely to require care
  - how the care needs of individuals will be assessed
  - how service needs identified will be incorporated into the planning process.

- **Services**
  - the client groups for whom they intend to arrange services
  - how priorities for arranging services are determined
  - how they intend to offer practical help, such as respite care, to carers
  - how they intend to develop domiciliary services

- **Quality**
  - the steps they are taking to ensure quality in providing and purchasing services
  - how they intend to monitor the quality of services they have purchased or provided
  - the setting up and role of inspection units
  - the setting up and role of complaints procedures

- **Consumer choice**
  - how they intend to increase consumer choice
  - how they intend to stimulate the development of a mixed economy of care

- **Resources**
  - the resource implications, both financial and human of planned future developments
  - how they intend to improve the cost effectiveness of services
  - their personnel and training strategy
- **Consultation**
  - their intentions for the required consultations
- **Publishing information**
  - what arrangements they intend to make to inform service users and their carers about services
  - how they intend to publish future community care plans

1.5 Under Section 7 of the Local Authority Social Services Act 1970, local authorities must exercise their social services functions under the guidance of the Secretary of State. Section 50 of the National Health Service and Community Care Act 1990 inserts a new Section 7A, which requires local authorities to exercise their social services functions "in accordance with such directions as may be given to them" by the Secretary of State. Accordingly, the Department of Health will advise the Secretary of State if it appears necessary to issue general directions to ensure that local authorities' plans are in line with national policies and priorities, and that implementation is proceeding at a reasonable pace, and the Secretary of State will use his powers to intervene where necessary (6).

The arrangement for the transfer of funds from the social security budget to local authorities, which is central to the objective of introducing a new funding structure for social care, has been postponed until April 1993. The rules governing financial assessment will be amended prior to the transfer and further guidance on these matters will be issued during 1992.

## 2. Services for Elderly People and People with Physical Disabilities

### 2.1 General Duty of Local Authorities

2.1.1 It is with the National Assistance Act 1948 that we must start if the overlapping and interlocking legislation in this area is to make sense. The language is now out of date, but Section 29(1) – as amended – provides the starting point for the law, with the following general duty of local authorities:

"A local authority may with the approval of the Secretary of State, and to such extent as he may direct in relation to persons ordinarily resident in the area of the local authority shall, make arrangements for promoting the welfare of persons aged eighteen or over who are blind, deaf or dumb or who suffer from mental disorder of any description and other persons aged eighteen or over who are substantially and permanently handicapped by illness, injury or congenital deformity or such other disabilities as may be prescribed by the minister."

2.1.2 The manifestation of this general duty has been subject to ministerial dictat and guidance, as well a subsequent legislation. Part III of the National Assistance Act 1948, which includes Section 29, is now covered by the definition of 'community care services' given in the National Health Service and Community Care Act 1990, and hence should be incorporated into the local authorities' community care plans.

### 2.2 Specific Services

2.2.1 The Chronically Sick and Disabled Persons Act 1970 and the National Health Service Act 1977 made this general duty more specific and mandatory. Section 1 of the Chronically Sick and Disabled Persons Act 1970 made it the duty of the local authority to inform themselves of the number of persons within their area to whom Section 29 of the National Assistance Act 1948 applies, and of the need for making by the authority of arrangements under that

108

Section for such persons. The local authority must also publish general information as to the services provided, and ensure that any person who uses the services is informed of any other of those services which are relevant to his needs. Section 2 of the 1970 Act then goes on to make it a duty, where a local authority are satisfied that it is necessary in order to meet the needs of a person to whom Section 29 of the 1948 Act applies, to make arrangements for all or any of the following

- the provision of practical assistance in the home

- the provision for, or assistance in obtaining, wireless, television, library or similar recreational facilities

- the provision of lectures, games, outings, or other recreational facilities outside the home or assistance in taking advantage of available educational facilities

- the provision of facilities for, or assistance in, travelling to and from home for the purpose of participating in any services provided under Section 29, or similar services

- the provision of assistance in arranging for the carrying out of any works of adaptation in the home or the provision of any additional facilities designed to secure greater safety, comfort or convenience

- facilitating the taking of holidays

- the provision of meals in the home or elsewhere

- the provision of, or assistance in obtaining, a telephone and any special equipment necessary to enable use of a telephone.

2.2.2  The National Health Service Act 1977, Schedule 8, went on to make it a duty to provide home help and the power to provide laundry facilities to a person who needs them because of illness, handicap or age. Services provided under this legislation are also included in the definition of community care services under the National Health Service and Community Care Act 1990, and must be included in community care plans.

## 2.3 Possible Services

2.3.1 Schedule 8 of The National Health Service Act 1977 also empowered local authorities to provide other possible services for the physically or mentally ill, including day centres, meals, social work support and residential accommodation, for the prevention of illness, for the care of people suffering from illness and for the aftercare of those who have suffered illness. Again, these services are defined as community care services under the 1990 Act and should be incorporated into community care plans.

2.3.2 The Health Services and Public Health Act 1968 empowered local authorities, with the approval of the Secretary of State, to make arrangements for the promotion of the welfare of old people.

The possible arrangements include

- provision of meals and recreation in the home and elsewhere

- facilities or assistance in travelling to and from the home for the purpose of participating in services provided by the authority or similar services

- assistance in finding suitable households for boarding elderly persons

- provision of visiting and advisory services and social work support

- provision of practical assistance in the home, including assistance in the carrying out of works of adaptation or the provision of any additional facilities designed to secure greater safety, comfort or convenience

- provision of wardens or contribution to the work of employing wardens on welfare functions in warden-assisted housing schemes

- provision of warden services for occupiers of private housing.

(Health Service and Public Health Act 1968, Section 45(1))

2.3.3 The possible services provided under the 1968 Act are included in the definition of community care services under the 1990 Act and must also, therefore, figure in community care plans.

2.3.4 A local authority may employ as its agent for the provision of welfare services for disabled persons or for promoting the welfare of old people any voluntary organisation or any person carrying on, professionally or by way of trade or business, activities which consist of or include the provision of services for any of the persons to whom Section 29 of the National Assistance Act 1948 applies. The agent must be an organisation or person appearing to the authority to be capable of providing the service to which the arrangements apply or capable of promoting the welfare of old people. (Section 30(1), National Assistance Act 1948 as amended by Section 42(6), National Health Service and Community Care Act 1990, and Section 45(3), Health Services and Public Health Act 1968 as amended by Section 42(7), National Health Service and Community Care Act).

2.3.5 It should be noted that it is under Schedule 8 of the National Health Service Act 1977 that schemes for the care of expectant mothers and under-fives who are not at state schools are also provided.

2.3.6 Section 2(1) of The Disabled Persons (Employment) Act 1958 also makes it possible for sheltered employment or training facilities to be provided for those whose disability makes them unlikely to obtain work.

2.3.7 District councils in the shire counties, which are not social services authorities, were also empowered to provide meals and recreation, in the home or elsewhere, by Schedule 9 of the Health and Social Services and Social Security Adjudications Act 1983.

## 2.4 Charging for Support Services

2.4.1 A local authority may charge for any or all of the specific and possible services considered above. The charges must be reasonable. However if a person satisfies the authority

111

providing the service that his means are insufficient, the authority shall not require him to pay more than it appears it is reasonably practicable for him to pay (Health and Social Services and Social Security Adjudications Act 1983, Section 17(1), (2) and (3)).

2.4.2 The Department of Health is to issue guidance on the powers and duties of local authorities to charge for personal social services, including care services (5). The Department expects local authorities to institute arrangements so that users of services of all types pay what they can reasonably afford towards their costs. But the provision of services, whether or not the local authority is under a statutory duty to make provision, should not be related to the ability of the user or their families to meet the costs. The assessment of financial means should, therefore, follow the assessment of need and decisions about service provision.

## 2.5 Other Supports for the Community Care of Adults

2.5.1 Cash benefits are not considered in detail in this book, but provide an essential part of the system of support for the care of adults in the community.

Particular reference should be made to

- **Contributory National Insurance benefits**

  - **statutory sick pay** (for up to 28 weeks in a period of incapacity for work)

  - **sickness benefit** (for those not entitled to statutory sick pay and incapable of work because of illness or disablement)

  - **invalidity pension and allowance** (which replaces statutory sick pay and sickness benefit after 28 weeks if incapacity continues)

  - **statutory maternity pay** (available, under certain conditions, from employers for the woman's first eighteen weeks off work)

  - **maternity allowance** (for women not entitled to statutory maternity pay, under certain conditions)

112

- **retirement pension** (payable to men at age 65 and women at age 60 provided they satisfy the contribution conditions)

- **graduated pension** (depending on contributions paid between 1961 and 1975, when graduated contributions ceased)

- **age addition** (payable to all pensioners aged 80 or over)

- **invalidity allowance** (which may be paid in addition to retirement pension)

• **Non-contributory benefits**

- **industrial injuries disablement benefit** (normally payable only if there is disablement assessed at 14% or more resulting from an industrial accident or pre-scribed industrial disease and can be increased by a constant attendance allowance and an exceptionally severe disablement allowance)

- **disability living allowance** (for those who need help with personal care, or help with getting around, or both)

- **disability working allowance** (for those who have an illness or disability that puts them at a disadvantage in getting a job and are starting to work or are already working)

- **attendance allowance** (payable to those aged over 65 who are severely disabled, either physically or men-tally, and who meet criteria for needing frequent attention)

- **invalid care allowance** (payable to people of working age who are unable to do full-time paid work because they care for a severely disabled person)

- **severe disablement allowance** (for people of working age who have been incapable of work for at least 28 weeks and who do not qualify for sickness or invalidity benefit)

113

- **The Independent Living Fund,** an independent charitable trust which provides financial help to enable severely disabled people to pay for the personal care and domestic support needed to maintain an independent life in the community, who

  – are aged between 16 and 74

  – are severely disabled

  – are receiving certain benefits for disabled people

  – cannot afford to pay for all the care needed and have savings of less than £8,000

  – are living alone or with another person who is unable to provide all the care needed (or are moving out of hospital or residential accommodation)

2.5.2 An employment service for people with disabilities is provided at job centres, the larger of which may have a Disablement Resettlement Officer, who can arrange for assessments, rehabilitation, retraining and help through special schemes. Under the Disabled Persons (Employment) Act 1944, the Secretary of State for Employment is required to keep and maintain a register of disabled people. Registration is voluntary and application to register can be made at job centres and careers offices. Before accepting registration the Disablement Resettlement Officer must determine that the applicant is disabled within the meaning of the Act, that the disability is likely to last for at least twelve months, that the applicant wishes to work and there is a reasonable prospect of his being able to do so. Registered disabled people are eligible to:

- employment under the quota scheme in open industry (currently 3% of the total work force of employers of 20 or more employees

- employment within the designated employment scheme (currently car park attendant and passenger electric lift attendant)

- sheltered employment (under the sheltered employment scheme, in sheltered workshops or with Remploy Ltd)

2.5.3 Community health services are intended to provide personal health care for people within the local community and to minimise the need for hospitalisation. They are the responsibility of District Health Authorities, and include

- health visitors, who are responsible for the promotion of good health through health education, advice and support and the prevention and detection of disease

- district nurses, who, working together with general practitioners, provide nursing care to all people living in the community, including those in residential homes

- maternity services, for expectant and nursing mothers and pre-school children

- chiropody services, with priority given to elderly and disabled people and expectant mothers

- the loan of equipment, for the continuation of medical treatment and nursing care outside hospital settings

- day hospitals, providing care and therapy to elderly patients, to enable them to remain in their homes whilst receiving treatment.

2.5.4 Travel assistance is available in the forms of

- concessionary fares for blind people on most forms of public transport

- assistance with the cost of travel to work of certain disabled people who are not able to use public transport

- concessionary fares for people of pensionable age

- the orange badge scheme, for motor vehicles driven by, or used for, the carriage of disabled persons, making them immune from many (but not all) parking restrictions.

# 3. Residential Care

## 3.1 Residential Care Provided by Local Authorities

3.1.1   The provision of residential accommodation for the elderly and for people with physical disabilities derives from Part III of the National Assistance Act 1948. For this reason it has often been referred to in the past as 'Part III accommodation'.

3.1.2   It is the duty of every local authority to provide residential accommodation for persons aged 18 or over who by reason of age, illness, disability, or any other circumstances are in need of care and attention which is not otherwise available to them and for expectant and nursing mothers who are in need of care and attention which is not otherwise available to them. It is the duty of local authorities to have regard to the welfare of all persons for whom accommodation is provided and to provide different kinds of accommodation appropriate to different categories of need (National Assistance Act 1948, Section 21(1) and (2) as amended by National Health Service and Community Care Act 1990, Section 42).

3.1.3   Local authorities may make rules as to the conduct of premises under its management but they are required to exercise their functions under the general guidance of the Secretary of State (National Assistance Act 1948, Section 23(1) and 35(2)).

3.1.4   A code drawn up by the Centre for Policy on Ageing called 'Home Life: A Code of Practice for Residential Care' (7) has taken on a semi-official status in recent years as a general guide to residential care. Guidance on residential care is primarily for use by inspection units (see below section 5 of this chapter) in evaluating the provision of residential care. There has now been a compilation of standards and guidance developed by the Social Services Inspectorate, in two documents:

- Guidance on Standards for Residential Homes for Elderly People (8)

116

- Guidance on Standards for Residential Homes for People with a Physical Disability (9)

3.1.5 The National Health Service and Community Care Act 1990 significantly affects the provision of accommodation under Part III of the 1948 Act, by enabling local authorities to pay for such accommodation to be provided commercially and by preventing the reception into Part III accommodation of a person already living in a privately registered or voluntary home, subject to regulations exempting certain classes of people. The 1990 legislation also significantly affects how the charges for accommodation are to be met (National Health Service and Community Care Act 1990, Sections 42, 43, 44 and 45).

3.1.6 These provisions are important to the government's pursuit of its objectives of promoting the development of a flourishing independent sector alongside good quality public services and of securing better value for taxpayers' money by introducing a new funding structure for social care.

## 3.2 Private Residential Care Homes

3.2.1 The law governing residential care homes is largely consolidated in the Registered Homes Act 1984.

3.2.2 A 'residential care home' is an establishment which provides or is intended to provide, whether for reward or not, residential accommodation with both board and personal care for persons in need of personal care by reason of old age, disablement, past or present dependence on alcohol or drugs, or past or present mental disorder (Registered Homes Act 1984, Section 1(1)).

3.2.3 Such homes must be registered with the local authority, and it is an offence not to register. The Registered Homes Act originally excluded homes providing care for fewer than four persons from registration, but this was amended by the Registered Homes (Amendment) Act in June 1991 so that such homes are covered by the legislation. (However it is not yet implemented, the autumn of 1992 being the

117

likely date.) Where the manager of a residential care home is not in control of it (whether as owner or otherwise), both the manager and the person in control are treated as carrying on the home and accordingly as required to be registered (Registered Homes Act 1984, Section 1(4) as amended by Registered Homes (Amendment) Act 1991, Section 3).

3.2.4 The certificate of registration states the maximum number of persons who may be resident, and the registration may also be subject to conditions regulating the age, sex or category of persons who may be received in the home. The registration authority may vary or add conditions, and it is an offence not to comply with them. The certificate must be kept affixed in a conspicuous place in the home (Registered Homes Act 1984, Section 5(3), (4), (5) and (6)).

3.2.5 The registration authority may refuse registration if satisfied that the person carrying on the home is not a fit person, the accommodation, staffing or equipment are not fit to be used for the purposes of the home, or the way in which it is intended to carry on the home is such as not to provide services or facilities reasonably required. Registration may also be cancelled on any of the above grounds, if the annual fee is not paid, or any offence under the Act is committed. There is provision for urgent cancellation of registration on application to a justice of the peace (Registered Homes Act 1984, Sections 9, 10 and 11).

3.2.6 The ordinary procedure for registration includes the right to make representations and there is a right of appeal to a Registered Homes Tribunal against a decision of a registration authority or an order made by a justice of the peace for the urgent cancellation of registration (Registered Homes Act 1984, Sections 12, 13, 14 and 15).

3.2.7 The Residential Care Homes Regulations 1984 set out the requirements as to the conduct of the homes. They are subject to inspection, which is considered in more detail below (see paragraph 5.2 of this chapter).

### 3.3 Nursing Homes

3.3.1 The law governing nursing homes is found in the Registered Homes Act 1984, as amended by the National Health Act 1980 and the Health and Social Services and Social Security Adjudications Act 1983.

3.3.2 A nursing home is defined as premises used or intended to be used for

- the reception of, and the provision of nursing services for, persons suffering from any sickness, injury or infirmity

- the reception of pregnant women or of women immediately after childbirth (referred to as 'maternity homes')

- the provision of all or any of the following services:
  - carrying out surgical procedures under anaesthesia
  - termination of pregnancies
  - endoscopy
  - haemodialysis or peritoneal dialysis
  - treatment by specially controlled techniques of medicine or surgery (including cosmetic surgery)

The Act specifically excludes a range of premises from the definition, including hospitals, mental nursing homes, sanitaria at schools, factory treatment rooms, doctors, dentists and chiropodists' surgeries and premises used for occupational health facilities (Registered Homes Act 1984, Section 21).

3.3.3 Nursing Homes must be registered with the Secretary of State, and it is an offence not to register. The Secretary of State has delegated responsibility for registration to the health authority. The certificate of registration states the maximum number of persons who may be resident, and the registration may also be subject to conditions regulating the age, sex and category of persons who may be received in the home. Conditions may be varied or added, and it is an offence not to comply with them. The certificate must

119

be kept in a conspicuous place in the home (Registered Homes Act 1984, Sections 23 and 29).

3.3.4 Registration may be refused if the applicant, an employee or proposed employee is not a fit person, the accommodation, staffing or equipment are not fit, the home or premises used in connection with it are improper or undesirable, or it contravenes Section 12(1) of the Health Services Act 1976 (which controls the construction of hospital buildings) or the home is not in the charge of a person who is either a registered medical practitioner or qualified nurse or, in the case of a maternity home, a certified midwife. Registration may also be cancelled on any of the above grounds, if the annual fee is not paid, or any offence under the Act is committed. There is provision for urgent cancellation of registration on application to a justice of the peace. The Health and Social Services and Social Security Adjudication Act 1983 has provided detailed procedures for cancellation of registration (Registered Homes Act 1984, Sections 25, 27, 28 and 30).

3.3.5 The ordinary procedure for registration includes the right to make representations and there is a right of appeal to a Registered Homes Tribunal against a decision of the Secretary of State or an order made by a justice of the peace for urgent cancellation of registration (Registered Homes Act 1984, Sections 31, 32, 33 and 34).

3.3.6 The Secretary of State has power to make regulations as to the conduct of nursing homes, and there is provision for inspections of them on such occasions and at such intervals as he may decide (Registered Homes Act 1984, Sections 26 and 35).

## 3.4 Reception Centres

### 3.4.1
The Department of Health have a duty to make provision whereby persons without a settled way of life may be influenced to lead a more settled way of life by means of reception centres which provide temporary board and lodgings (National Assistance Act 1948, Section 17(1)).

### 3.4.2
This duty may be discharged by direction given to, and in consultation with, local authorities. The local authority may recover its costs from the Department of Health (National Assistance Act 1948, Section 17(2)).

### 3.4.3
The DoH may make contributions to voluntary organisations for maintaining centres for purposes similar to reception centres (National Assistance Act 1948, Section 17(4)).

## 3.5 Compulsory Admission to Residential Care

### 3.5.1
The National Assistance Act 1948 provides for the compulsory removal from home to a hospital or other suitable place of certain persons for whom it is necessary to secure care and attention. Section 47 of the Act applies to persons who

- are suffering from grave chronic disease or being aged, infirm or physically incapacitated, are living in insanitary conditions, and

- are unable to devote to themselves, and are not receiving from other persons, proper care and attention (National Assistance Act 1948, Section 47(1)).

### 3.5.2
The power to apply for compulsory removal lies with the local authority on receiving medical confirmation from a person called the "proper officer", who will normally be the community physician. If the proper officer certifies in writing to the appropriate authority that he is satisfied after thorough inquiry and consideration that in the interests of any such person or for preventing injury to the health of, or serious nuisance to, other persons, it is necessary to remove any such person the authority may apply to the magistrates' court (National Assistance Act 1948, Section 47(2)).

121

3.5.3   7 days' notice of the application prior to the hearing should be given to the person to be removed and to the manager of the proposed accommodation, unless the manager comes to court to give oral evidence that suitable accommodation is available (National Assistance Act 1948, Section 47(7)).

3.5.4   The community physician must give oral evidence of facts presented in the written report, and if satisfied of the allegations in the certificate and that it is expedient to do so, the court may order the removal of the person to a suitable hospital or other place for a period not exceeding three months. The order can be renewed for further periods of three months by the magistrates as many times as necessary (National Assistance Act 1948, Section 47(3) and (4)).

3.5.5   In an emergency, it is possible for an order for the removal of any such person to be made without the required notices to the person and the manager of the proposed accommodation. The application may be to a magistrates' court or a single justice, and has to be certified by the community physician and another registered medical practitioner that in their opinion it is necessary in the interests of the person to remove him without delay. Such an emergency order gives power to detain the person for up to 3 weeks, during which a further application can be made with 7 days notice (National Assistance (Amendment) Act 1951, Section 1).

3.5.6   At any time after the expiration of six clear weeks from the making of an order, an application may be made to the court by or on behalf of the person in respect of whom the order was made, for revocation of the order. If in the circumstances it appears expedient to do so, the court may revoke the order (National Assistance Act 1948, Section 47(6)).

3.5.7   The person can only be detained against his will in the place specified in the order; any variation requires a magistrates' court order. If the compulsory detention lapses the person is free to leave, or may of course remain voluntarily. A right of appeal against a magistrates' court order lies to the Crown Court.

## 3.6 Protection of Property

3.6.1 When a person is admitted as a patient to a hospital, or is admitted to accommodation provided under Part III of the National Assistance Act 1948, or is removed to any other place under an order made under Section 47 of the National Assistance Act 1948, and it appears that there is a danger of loss or damage to any movable property, and no suitable arrangements have been made to protect the property, the local authority have a duty to take reasonable steps to prevent or mitigate loss or damage (National Assistance Act 1948, Section 48(1)).

3.6.2 The local authority only have an obligation where it is aware of the circumstances, and in order to discharge their duty they can enter the place of residence and deal with any moveable property in any way that is reasonable and necessary (National Assistance Act 1948, Section 48(2)).

## 4. Care Management and Assessment

### 4.1 Assessment

4.1.1 Where it appears to a local authority that any person for whom they may provide or arrange the provision of community care services may be in need of any such services it has a duty

- to carry out an assessment of his needs for those services; and

- having regard to the results of that assessment, then to decide whether his needs call for the provision by them of any such services.

(National Health Service and Community Care Act 1990, Section 47(1))

4.1.2 Although this duty relates only to community care services as defined by the Act (see paragraph 1.3 above of this chapter), the policy guidance of the Department of Health advises: "However, the aim of assessment should be to ensure that all needs for care services are considered". (10)

123

Section 47(3) of the Act requires social services departments to bring apparent housing and health care needs to the attention of the local housing authority or the District Health Authority and to invite them to assist in making the assessment. In making any decision as to the provision of the services needed for the person in question, the local authority must take into account any services which are likely to be made available for him by the housing or health authorities (National Health Service and Community Care Act 1990, Section 47(3)).

4.1.3 The Disabled Persons (Services, Consultation and Representation) Act 1986 has been partially implemented, and links with the National Health Service and Community Care Act 1990 in specific ways. In accordance with Section 47(2) of the 1990 Act, if, at any time during their assessment, any person appears to be a disabled person within the meaning of the 1986 Act, the local authority

- shall proceed to make such a decision as to the services he requires as is mentioned in Section 4 of the Disabled Persons (Services, Consultation and Representation) Act 1986, without his requesting them to do so under that section; and

- shall inform him that they will be doing so and of his rights under that Act.

What Section 4 of the 1986 Act states is that the local authority must assess the needs of a disabled person for any of the services listed in Section 2 of the Chronically Sick and Disabled Persons Act 1970 – see above paragraph 2.2.1 of this chapter – if asked by the disabled person or his authorised representative or carer. What this means is that there is no need to duplicate the assessment by waiting for the disabled person to request an assessment. A disabled person is one to whom Section 29 of the National Assistance Act 1948 applies (see above paragraph 2.1.1 of this chapter).

4.1.4 The National Health Service and Community Care Act 1990 provides for services to be provided without assessment where they are required as a matter of urgency.

124

Where this happens, an assessment must be carried out as soon as practicable afterwards (National Health Service and Community Care Act 1990, Section 47(5) and (6)).

4.1.5 The community care plans should include arrangements for the publication of readily accessible information about care services and the assessment procedures so that users and carers can participate in the assessment of their care needs and exercise genuine choice in the making of arrangements for meeting those needs. The Department of Health advises (11) that assessment arrangements should normally include an initial screening process to determine the appropriate form of assessment, as some people may need advice and assistance which do not call for a formal assessment, others may require only a limited or specialist assessment of specific needs, others may have urgent needs which require an immediate response. Voluntary organisations may have a role in providing expert advice in assessment and it will be possible to include assessment of needs in social services departments' contract arrangement with such specialist agencies. Authorities are also advised to promote the involvement of people who can assist service users and carers during assessment, including interpreters, both to help with communication and to explain cultural needs.

4.1.6 The assessment will need to take into account the support provided by families, friends and neighbours. The Department of Health advises (12) that such carers should feel that the overall provision of care is a shared responsibility between them and the statutory authorities and that the relationship between them is one of mutual support, and that carers who feel they need community care services in their own right can ask for a separate assessment.

4.1.7 It is expected that as a matter of good practice General Practitioners will wish to make a full contribution to assessment, and it is part of a GP's terms of service to give advice to enable patients to avail themselves of services provided by a local authority. Appropriate medical and nursing advice should always be sought when admission to residential or nursing home care is being considered. The 1990 Act requires social services departments to obtain health authority consent before placing users in nursing homes, except in cases of urgency, under Section 47(5). (13).

## 4.2 Care Plans

4.2.1 Once needs have been assessed, the services to be provided or arranged and the objectives of any intervention should be agreed in the form of a care plan. The aim should be to secure the most cost-effective package of services that meets the user's care needs, taking account of the user's and carer's own preferences.

4.2.2 Care management will play a key part in achieving the government's objectives for community care by:

- ensuring that the resources available (including resources transferred in due course from social security) are used in the most effective way to meet individual care needs

- restoring and maintaining independence by enabling people to live in the community wherever possible

- working to prevent or to minimise the effects of disability and illness in people of all ages

- treating those who need services with respect and providing equal opportunities for all

- promoting individual choice and self-determination and building on existing strengths and care resources; and

- promoting partnership between users, carers and service providers in all sectors, together with organisations of and for each group (14).

4.2.3 The Department of Health's guidance suggests that the pursuit of these objectives implies the following order of preference in constructing care packages:

- support for the user in his or her own home including day and domiciliary care, respite care, the provision of

126

disability equipment and adaptations to accommodation as necessary

- a move to more suitable accommodation which might be sheltered or very sheltered housing, together with the provision of social services support

- a move to another private household, i.e. to live with relatives or friends or as part of an adult fostering scheme

- residential care

- nursing home care

- long-stay care in hospital (15)

4.2.4 Care managers should assume some or all the responsibility for purchasing services necessary to implement a care plan. Care managers can come from a number of professions and will vary according to the needs of service users, and need not necessarily be employed by a statutory authority. Their role should not include being involved in direct service delivery, but they should act in effect as brokers for services across the statutory and independent sectors. Where service users are not provided with a single care manager, there should always be a nominated worker to act as the primary point of contact in resolving any difficulties. The care manager must be distinct from the keyworker, who carries the main service providing role (16).

4.2.5 This split between the "purchaser/commissioner" of services and the "provider" of services at the 'micro' level where services are being arranged for individuals, reflects the split at a 'macro' level. The Griffiths Report (1) proposed that local authorities should be the commissioners and purchasers of care services and this was endorsed in the White Paper "Caring for People" (2). The same approach is central to the reforms of the National Health Service as set out in the White Paper "Working for Patients" (17). Thus the statutory authorities are to become "enabling authorities", identifying the needs for care among their populations, planning how best to meet those needs, setting overall strategies, priorities and targets, commissioning and purchasing as well as providing necessary services and ensuring the quality and value of those services. The Department of Health has suggested possible models for the development of purchaser, commissioner and provider roles (18). This conception of the delivery of community care will become increasingly important when funds are transferred from the Department of Social Security to the local authorities and social services departments will need to commission not only residential care but also nursing home care, day care and packages of domiciliary care, provided in an increasingly mixed economy of care by the private and voluntary sectors and by the local authorities themselves.

## 4.3 Review of Care Needs

4.3.1 Care needs, for which services are being provided, should be reviewed at regular intervals. The timing of the review should be stated in the original care plan, but may take place earlier if it is clear that community care needs have changed. The review should be undertaken by someone not involved in direct service provision, such as a care manager (19).

4.3.2 The type of review will vary according to need but all those involved in the original care planning should be consulted. Large scale review meetings should rarely be necessary. All relevant agencies, service users and carers should be notified of the results of the review (20).

## 4.4 Confidentiality of Health and Personal Social Services Information

4.4.1 Any consultations and collaborations in respect of care assessment, care planning or care reviews need to have regard to codes of practice and the law in respect of confidentiality. Proper assessment, the design of appropriate packages of care and the arrangement of services, may depend on agencies being able to share information. The need for this should be explained to the service user and his or her written consent first obtained (21).

4.4.2 The Data Protection Act 1984, the Access to Personal Files Act 1987 and the Access to Health Records Act 1990 will affect the use authorities make of information they receive or hold, and the circumstances in which it can be disclosed. Detailed guidance is given in circulars LAC(87)10, LAC(88)16, LAC(88)17, HC(FP)(88)22 and LAC(89)2.

## 4.5 Guidance on Good Practice

4.5.1 The Social Services Inspectorate of the Department of Health has published a Practitioners' Guide, and a Manager's Guide in respect of care management and assessment (HMSO 1991). The former sets out good practice, and the latter deals with organisational and training issues.

4.5.2 The guidance is structured around the seven core tasks and stages involved in arranging care for someone in need

- publishing information
- determining the level of assessment
- assessing need
- implementing the care plan
- monitoring
- reviewing

# 5. Inspection of Community Care Services

## 5.1 Introduction

5.1.1 The inspection of private and voluntary residential care homes has been long established. The National Health Service and Community Care Act 1990 has introduced provisions for the inspection of premises used for community care services, including local authorities' own residential care homes. The White Paper (2) proposed that free-standing inspection units should be set up within local authorities which would put the inspections of residential care in the public, private and voluntary sectors on a common footing.

5.1.2  The Department of Health's guidance (22) states that units will be concerned in the first place to

- evaluate the quality of care provided and the quality of life experienced in private and voluntary residential care homes and in local authority establishments similarly providing board and personal care

- ensure that a consistent approach is taken to inspection of public, private and voluntary provision

- respond to the demands and opportunities for quality control created by the growth in contracted-out service provision

- undertake their duties even-handedly, efficiently and cost-effectively.

5.1.3  Units may also support and assist in the development of quality assurance programmes, provide a source of advice on the setting of standards for contracted-out services, contribute to the quality control systems established to check that those standards are achieved and undertake the inspection of the authority's domiciliary and other non-residential services (23).

## 5.2 Inspection of Registered Residential Care Homes

5.2.1  The statutory basis for such inspections is provided by Section 17 of the Registered Homes Act 1984. An authorised person may at all times enter and inspect any premises which are used, or which that person has reasonable cause to believe to be used, for the purposes of a residential care home (Section 17(1) and (2)).

5.2.2  The powers of inspection include power to inspect any records required to be kept in accordance with the Residential Care Homes Regulations 1984, and at the intervals and on the occasions prescribed in the Regulations (Section 17(3) and (4)).

5.2.3  A person who proposes to exercise any power of entry or inspection must produce some duly authenticated document showing his authority to do so, if requested (Section 17(5)).

5.2.4 Any person who obstructs an authorised person in the exercise of any such power shall be guilty of an offence (Registered Homes Act 1984, Section 17(6)).

## 5.3 Inspection of Premises used for the Provision of Community Care Services

5.3.1 The statutory basis for such inspections is provided by Section 48 of the National Health Service and Community Care Act 1990. An authorised person may at any reasonable time enter and inspect any premises (other than premises in respect of which any person is registered under the Registered Homes Act 1984) in which community care services are or are proposed to be provided by a local authority, whether directly or under arrangements made with another person (National Health Service and Community Care Act 1990, Section 48(1)).

5.3.2 An authorised person inspecting premises may

- make such examination into the state and management of the premises and the facilities and services provided therein as he thinks fit

- inspect any records (in whatever form they are held) relating to the premises, or any person for whom community care services have been or are to be provided there, and

- require the owner of, or any person employed in, the premises to furnish him with such information as he may request.

The authorised person has a right of access to any computer and associated apparatus or material used in connection with records, and may require reasonable assistance with their operation (National Health Service and Community Care Act 1990, Section 48(2) and (3)).

5.3.3 The authorised person may also interview any person residing at the premises, in private, for the purpose of investigating any complaint or if he has reason to believe that the community care services being provided there for that person are not satisfactory; and he may examine any

131

such person in private if he is a registered medical practitioner. Only a registered medical practitioner may inspect medical records (National Health Service and Community Care Act 1990, Section 48(4) and (5)).

5.3.4 An authorised person exercising the power of entry must produce some duly authenticated document showing his authority to do so, if requested. Any person who intentionally obstructs another in the exercise of that power shall be guilty of an offence (National Health Service and Community Care Act 1990, Section 48(6) and (7)).

## 5.4 Inspection Processes

5.4.1 Responsibility for the organisation and management of inspection units and for safeguarding their independence should rest with the Director of Social Services (24).

5.4.2 Local authorities' procedures should set out the arrangements to ensure that where the outcome of an inspection calls for remedial or other action, that it is taken, and that there are rules concerning the preparation and monitoring of reports, including time limits (25).

5.4.3 An annual report of the work of an inspection unit should be presented to the Social Services Committee. The Department of Health's guidance (26) outlines a possible format for the annual report, and advises that, where individual homes or other services are identified in annual reports, they should be anonymised (subject to legal advice to the contrary), except where it would have the effect of denying public access to the report under the Local Government (Access to Information) Act 1985.

5.4.4 Inspection units are to be supported by an advisory committee in each authority. The committee should serve as a forum for the exchange of views between the authority, its officers and service providers who are subject to inspection or other quality control measures undertaken by the inspection unit and service users; and to provide mutual support. It is for the authority to determine membership, terms of reference and mode of operation,

132

but the opportunity should be taken to involve users or carers. The advisory committees should not have executive powers. The Department of Health's guidance provides a model framework for advisory committees (27).

5.4.5 The Social Services Inspectorate will monitor the progress of inspection units, and the guidance on standards, referred to in paragraph 3.1.4 above, and provide inspection units with assistance in developing standards for inspection.

## 6. Complaints Procedures

### 6.1 The Legal Basis of Complaints Procedures

6.1.1 Section 50 of the National Health Service and Community Care Act 1990 inserts a new section – Section 7B – into the Local Authority Social Services Act 1970. Section 7B authorises the Secretary of State to require local authorities to establish a procedure for considering any representations (including any complaints) which are made to them by a qualifying individual, or anyone acting on his behalf, in relation to the discharge of, or any failure to discharge, any of their social services functions in respect of that individual.

6.1.2 Complaints must be made by and must be in respect of a 'qualifying individual', or be made by someone acting on behalf of that individual. A person is a qualifying individual if

- a local authority has a power or a duty to provide, or to secure the provision of, a social service for him; and

- his need or possible need for such a service has (by whatever means) come to the attention of the authority.

6.1.3 The consequence of this legal basis of complaints or representations is that any of a general nature, unrelated to an individual case, are likely to fall outside the statutory definition. Similarly, anonymous complaints are likely to fall outside the legal framework. However, it is open to authorities to deal with complaints not covered by Section 7B at their discretion.

133

6.1.4 In the exercise of the powers conferred by Section 7B(3), the Secretary of State has given directions to local authorities – the Complaints Procedure Directions 1990.

## 6.2 The Required Procedures

6.2.1 Where a local authority receives representations from any complainant, they shall try to resolve the matter informally.

6.2.2 If the matter cannot be resolved to the satisfaction of the complainant, the local authority shall give or send to him an explanation of the procedure set out in the Directions and ask him to submit a written representation if he wishes to proceed.

6.2.3 The local authority shall offer assistance and guidance to the complainant on the use of this procedure, or give advice on where he may obtain it.

6.2.4 A written representation becomes a 'registered' complaint and the local authority must consider it, and formulate a response within 28 days of its receipt, or if this is not possible, explain to the complainant within that period why it is not possible and tell him when he can expect a response, which shall in any event be within 3 calendar months of receipt of the representation.

6.2.5 The local authority shall notify in writing the result of their consideration to:
- the complainant
- the person on whose behalf the representations were made, unless the local authority consider that that person is not able to understand it or it would cause him unnecessary distress
- any other person who the local authority considers has sufficient interest in the case.

6.2.5 If the complainant informs the authority within 28 days of the above notification that he is dissatisfied with the result and wishes the matter to be referred to a panel for review, the local authority shall appoint a panel to consider the matter which must be referred to it.

134

6.2.6 A panel of three people, at least one of whom shall be an independent person, shall meet within 28 days of the receipt of the complainant's request for review to consider the matter together with any oral or written submissions as the complainant or the local authority wish the panel to consider. The Chair should be an independent person. Complainants should be notified in writing at least 10 days beforehand of the time and venue of the meeting and be invited to attend. Complainants should also be informed of the name and status of the panel members, which officers of the authority will be present, and of their right to make written and oral submissions. They should be told of their entitlement to be accompanied by another person who can be present at the whole meeting and to speak on their behalf if they so wish. The authority may need to consider what provision should be made for complainants whose first language is not English or those who may have mobility problems or special communication needs.

6.2.7 The review meeting should be conducted as informally as possible. The chair of the panel should open the meeting by explaining its purpose and proposed procedures and with a reminder about confidentiality. The complainant (or a person accompanying him or her) should be given the opportunity to make an oral submission before the authority's representative does. Other people may attend to make oral submissions if requested to do so by the complainant, subject to the consent of the panel, but will normally only be allowed to be present for that part of the meeting.

6.2.8 The panel shall decide on its recommendations and record them in writing within 24 hours of the end of its meeting, and shall send written copies of their recommendations to

- the local authority
- the complainant
- if appropriate, the person on whose behalf the representations were made, and
- any other person whom the local authority considers has sufficient interest in the case.

6.2.9 The panel must record the reasons for their recommend-ations in writing, and the local authority must consider what action to take, notify the persons listed above of their decisions and of their reasons for taking that decision and of any action which they have taken or propose to take, within 28 days of the date of the panel's recommendations.

(Complaints Procedures Directions 1990 and Chapter 6 of the Department of Health's guidance (4))

## 6.3 Publicity, Co-ordination and Monitoring of Complaints Procedures

6.3.1 The Act requires that local authorities shall give such publicity as they consider appropriate to their complaints procedures (Local Authority Social Services Act 1970 – as amended – Section 7 B(4)).

6.3.2 The Complaints Procedure Directions 1990 require the local authority to appoint one of their officers to assist the authority in the co-ordination of all aspects of their consideration of representations, and to ensure that all members or officers involved in the handling of representations are familiar with the procedures (Direction 4(1) and 4(2)).

6.3.3 Direction 9 also requires the local authority to keep a record of each representation received, the outcome of each representation, and whether there was compliance with the time limits specified in the directions. The Department of Health's guidance (28) states that an annual report dealing with the operation of the complaints procedure should be presented to the Social Services Committee, and that all or part of the periodic reports made to the Council or Social Services Committee should be open to inspection by members of the public under the terms of the Local Government (Access to Information) Act 1985, anonymised where necessary to ensure there is no breach of confidentiality.

## 6.4 Links with Other Procedures

6.4.1 The representation procedure in respect of children was considered in the previous chapter of this book (in section 9), where it was noted that the complaints procedures required for other local authority social services functions are broadly comparable, and may be operated within the same structure. The main difference is that the Children Act 1989 requires the involvement of an independent person at each stage of consideration of a representation or a complaint. The Department of Health's guidance (29) suggests that the two procedures might merge at the panel review stage, where independent persons also become part of the procedure for adults.

6.4.2 Wherever possible the service providers should handle complaints about services provided in the voluntary or private sectors with financial support from the local authority. Registered residential care homes are, in any case, required by law to have a procedure for investigating complaints. Where a complainant is dissatisfied with the response to a complaint dealt with by a voluntary or private sector service provider and refers the matter to the social services department, the Department of Health guidance (30) advises that the complaint should be treated as a registered complaint.

6.4.3 Where a registered complaint is lodged by a person being cared for in a nursing home under the terms of a contractual arrangement made between the home and a local authority, the authority should pass a copy of the complaint to the health authority registration officer responsible for the registration and inspection of the home. The procedure for dealing with such cases should be agreed between the two authorities (31).

6.4.4 The complaints procedure should not affect in any way the right of an individual or organisation to approach a local councillor for advice or assistance.

6.4.5 The Mental Health Act Commission has responsibility for overseeing the detention and treatment of compulsorily detained patients and a general responsibility for the care, treatment and aftercare of all mentally disordered people, who, together with their carers, may complain to the Commission. Its responsibilities are considered in the next chapter of this book.

## References

1. Department of Health (1988) "Community Care: Agenda for Action", HMSO, London.

2. Department of Health (1989) "Caring for People: Community Care in the Next Decade and Beyond", HMSO, London.

3. N.I.S.W. (1988), "Residential Care: A Positive Choice", HMSO, London, Volume 1.

4. Department of Health (1990) "Community Care in the Next Decade and Beyond", HMSO, London.

5. Department of Health (1990) "Community Care in the Next Decade and Beyond", HMSO, London, Paragraph 3.31

6. Department of Health (1990) "Community Care in the Next Decade and Beyond", HMSO, London, Paragraph 2.21.

7. Centre for Policy on Ageing (1984) "Home Life: A Code of Practice for Residential Care".

8. Department of Health (1990) "Guidance on Standards for Residential Homes for Elderly People", HMSO, London.

9. Department of Health (1990) "Guidance on Standards for Residential Homes for People with a Physical Disability", HMSO, London.

10. Department of Health (1990) "Community Care in the Next Decade and Beyond", HMSO, London, Paragraph 3.32.

11. Department of Health (1990) "Community Care in the Next Decade and Beyond", HMSO, London, Paragraphs 3.20, 3.49 and 3.23.

12. Department of Health (1990) "Community Care in the Next Decade and Beyond", HMSO, London, Paragraphs 3.28 and 3.29.

13. Department of Health (1990) "Community Care in the Next Decade and Beyond", HMSO, London, Paragraphs 3.48 and 3.39 and 3.38.

14. Department of Health (1990) "Community Care in the Next Decade and Beyond", HMSO, London, Paragraph 3.3.

15. Department of Health (1990) "Community Care in the Next Decade and Beyond", HMSO, London, Paragraph 3.24.

16. Department of Health (1990) "Community Care in the Next Decade and Beyond", HMSO, London, Paragraphs 3.10, 3.11, 3.12 and 3.13.

17. Department of Health (1987) "Working for Patients", HMSO, London.

18. Department of Health (1991) "Implementing Community Care: Purchaser, Commissioner and Provider Rules", HMSO, London.

19. Department of Health (1990) "Community Care in the Next Decade and Beyond", HMSO, London, Paragraph 3.51.

20. Department of Health (1990) "Community Care in the Next Decade and Beyond", HMSO, London, Paragraph 3.53.

21. Department of Health (1990) "Community Care in the Next Decade and Beyond", HMSO, London, Paragraph 3.50.

22. Department of Health (1990) "Community Care in the Next Decade and Beyond", HMSO, London, Paragraph 5.6.

23. Department of Health (1990) "Community Care in the Next Decade and Beyond", HMSO, London, Paragraph 5.14.

24. Department of Health (1990) "Community Care in the Next Decade and Beyond", HMSO, London, Paragraph 5.7.

25. Department of Health (1990) "Community Care in the Next Decade and Beyond", HMSO, London, Paragraph 5.16.

26. Department of Health (1990) "Community Care in the Next Decade and Beyond", HMSO, London, Paragraph 5.18, Annex A and 5.19.

27. Department of Health (1990) "Community Care in the Next Decade and Beyond", HMSO, London, Paragraphs 5.20, 5.21, 5.22 and Annex B.

28. Department of Health (1990) "Community Care in the Next Decade and Beyond", HMSO, London, Paragraphs 6.24 and 6.25.

29. Department of Health (1990) "Community Care in the Next Decade and Beyond", HMSO, London, Paragraph 6.20.

30. Department of Health (1990) "Community Care in the Next Decade and Beyond", HMSO, London, Paragraph 6.31.

31. Department of Health (1990) "Community Care in the Next Decade and Beyond", HMSO, London, Paragraph 6.32.

## Chapter Three

# The Care and Control of People with Problems of Mental Health

## Introduction

"The foundations of our current policies were laid in professional and government pronouncements in the 1950s and early 1960s. The Royal Commission on the Law relating to Mental Illness and Mental Deficiency (1954-57), found that their witnesses were 'generally in favour of a shift of emphasis from hospital care to community care' and in the light of this the Commission recommended 'a general reorientation away from institutional care in its present form and towards community care' (HMSO 1957)." (1)

The large mental illness hospitals began to contract during the 1960s, and community care remained the cornerstone of government policy, as reflected in two White Papers – one in 1971 'Better Services for the Mentally Handicapped' (2) and one in 1975 'Better Services for the Mentally Ill' (3). However, economic recession and limited local authority resources made a real shift from institutional to community care and a true realisation of better services a slow process.

The Royal Commission of 1954-57 led to the most significant and radical legislation for the management of mental disorder – the Mental Health Act 1959. In 1976 this legislation was reviewed (4), and this review resulted in the Mental Health Act 1983, which consolidates the law relating to people with problems of mental health contained in the Mental Health Act 1959 and the Mental Health (Amendment) Act 1982. The main provisions of the 1983 Act came into force on 30 September 1983, and it is this legislation which continues to be the base of the law in this area. Under Section 118 of the Mental Health Act 1983, the Secretary of State for Health and the Secretary of State for Wales are required to prepare a Code of Practice. The Code was published in May 1990, and together with the Act, provides the substance of this chapter.

However, the issue of resources goes on alongside changes in the law. In 1981 the Government published a consultative document 'Care in the Community' (5) on ways in which appropriate community services might be developed, but by 1989 was forced to state in the White Paper 'Caring for People': "The Government recognises ... that progress has not been uniformly satisfactory and there are legitimate concerns that in some places hospital beds have been closed before better, alternative facilities were fully in place". (6) Hence, the government issued a circular (HC(90)23/LASSL(90)11) requiring health authorities to introduce, from 1 April 1991, the care programme approach for the provision of community care for people with a mental illness and asks social services authorities to collaborate with health authorities in introducing this approach and, as resources allow, to continue to expand social care services to patients being treated in the community. The National Health Service and Community Care Act 1990, Section 50, inserts a new Section – Section 7E – into the Local Authority Social Services Act 1970, which makes it possible for the Secretary of State to make a specific grant to local authorities for services for people with a mental illness (including dementia, whatever its cause). This has been introduced, from 1991, as a recurrent annual contribution (initially for up to three years) to social services authorities' revenue spending.

This chapter does not consider patients concerned in criminal proceedings or under sentence, as such a consideration fits more appropriately in the next chapter on offenders.

## 1. Services for People with Problems of Mental Health

### 1.1 Services for Children

1.1.1 As was noted in Chapter 1, a key principle of the Children Act 1989 is that provision for various children should be integrated into the overall framework of services for children. It is to that legislation, therefore, that one must turn for the legislative base of services for children.

1.1.2 The Children Act 1989 lays a general duty on every local authority to safeguard and promote the welfare of children who are in need; need is defined in terms of development, health and disability, which are further defined thus:

- 'development' means physical, intellectual, emotional, social or behavioural development

- 'health' means physical or mental health

- a child is disabled if he is blind, deaf or dumb or suffers from mental disorder of any kind or is substantially and permanently handicapped by illness, injury or congenital deformity or such other disability as may be prescribed. (Children Act 1989, Section 17(1), (10) and (11))

1.1.3 The support for families and children in need and the services provided, described in Chapter 1, relate equally to children with problems of mental health.

1.1.4 Provision for children with special educational needs is covered by the Education Act 1981. A child has special educational needs if he has a learning difficulty which calls for special educational provision to be made for him.

A learning difficulty exists if:

- he has a significantly greater difficulty in learning than the majority of children of his age; or

- he has a disability which either prevents or hinders him from making use of educational facilities of a kind generally provided in schools, within the area of the local authority, for children of his age; or

- he is under the age of 5 years and is, or would be if special educational provisions were not made for him, likely to fall within either of the two categories above when over that age.

The local education authority has a duty to identify those children whose special needs require special provision and to provide special educational provision.

1.1.5 The Children Act 1989 lays a duty on health and local education authorities which provide, or intend to provide, accommodation for a child for a consecutive period of more than three months to notify the responsible local authority where the child usually lives. The responsible local authority must take such steps as are reasonably practicable to enable them to decide whether the child's welfare is adequately safeguarded and promoted while he stays in the accommodation and they must consider whether they should exercise any of their functions under the Act (Children Act 1989, Section 85(1), (2), (3) and (4)).

1.1.6 The responsible local authority must also be informed when the child leaves the accommodation provided. If he is under twenty-one when he leaves, he may qualify for advice and assistance from the local authority (Children Act 1989, Section 85(2) and 24(4) and (5)).

1.1.7 Similarly, the persons carrying on residential care homes, mental nursing homes and nursing homes must notify the local authority if a child is, or is intended to be, accommodated for three consecutive months, and must be notified when he leaves. The authority has the same functions and the child may qualify for advice and assistance as in the previous paragraphs (Children Act 1989, Section 86(1) and (2) and Section 24(2), (4) and (5)).

## 1.2 Services for Adults

1.2.1 As was noted in chapter 2, the National Health Service and Community Care Act 1990 in its definition of 'community care services' includes provisions under Section 117 of the Mental Health Act 1983. Section 117 imposes a duty on the District Health Authority and the social services department to provide, in co-operation with relevant voluntary agencies, aftercare services for certain patients. The duty continues until the two authorities are satisfied that the person no longer needs such a service. These services must be included in the local authority's community care plan.

1.2.2 As was noted in Chapter 2 – at paragraph 2.1.1 – Section 29(1) of the National Assistance Act 1948, as amended, includes "people who suffer from mental disorder of any description and other persons who are substantially and permanently handicapped by illness, injury or congenital deformity" amongst those whose welfare a local authority has a general duty to promote. Therefore, the specific

144

services and possible services that must be provided for elderly people and people with physical disabilities under the Chronically Sick and Disabled Person Act 1970 and the National Health Service Act 1977 are similarly available for people with problems of mental health (see chapter 2, paragraphs 2.2 and 2.3.1).

1.2.3 Elderly people with mental health problems may additionally be covered by the possible services provided under the Health Service and Public Health Act 1968 (see chapter 2, paragraph 2.3.2). Provisions in respect of compulsory admission to residential care are detailed in chapter 2, paragraph 3.5.

1.2.4 Cash benefits – outlined in paragraph 2.5 of chapter 2 – may in some instances also apply to people with problems of mental health.

1.2.5 Other provisions for the inspection of premises and for the making of representations which were considered in chapter 2, apply similarly to services for people with problems of mental health which are provided as community care services.

## 1.3 Services under the Mental Health Act 1983

1.3.1 What follows in this Chapter is the law relating to the care and control of people with problems of mental health, as provided under the Mental Health Act 1983.

1.3.2 Before considering specific aspects of the legislation, it should be noted that the Code of Practice sets out the following broad principles in respect of those being assessed for possible admission under the Act or to whom the Act applies; they should:

- receive respect for and consideration of their individual qualities and diverse backgrounds - social, cultural, ethnic and religious;
- have their needs taken fully into account though it is recognised that, within available resources, it may not always be practicable to meet them;

- be delivered any necessary treatment or care in the least controlled and segregated facilities practicable;

- be treated or cared for in such a way that promotes to the greatest practicable degree their self-determination and personal responsibility consistent with their needs and wishes;

- be discharged from any order under the Act to which they are subject immediately it is no longer necessary.

## 2.  Definitions of Mental Disorder

### 2.1  General

2.1.1  Mental illness is not defined in the legislation.  This is a matter for clinical judgment.  The legislation refers to "the reception, care and treatment of mentally disordered patients".

2.1.2  By virtue of the general definition of mental disorder, the Act applies to people with learning difficulties, but only when associated with severe behaviour problems.

2.1.3  Promiscuity or other immoral conduct, sexual deviancy or dependence on drugs or alcohol do not in themselves constitute mental disorder (Mental Health Act 1983, Section 1(3)).

### 2.2  Definitions

2.1.1  *Mental disorder* means "mental illness, arrested or incomplete development of mind, psychopathic disorder and any other disorder or disability of mind".  A general diagnosis of mental disorder is sufficient for admission for assessment under Sections 2 and 4 and for the use of Sections 135 and 136 (see below) (Mental Health Act 1983, Section 1(2)).

2.2.2  In order for a patient to be admitted for treatment or to guardianship one or more forms of specific mental disorder must be present which the Act defines.  They are:

146

- *Severe mental impairment*, which is "a state of arrested or incomplete development of mind which includes severe impairment of intelligence and social functioning and is associated with abnormally aggressive or seriously irresponsible conduct ...".

- *Mental impairment*, which is "a state of arrested or incomplete development of mind (not amounting to severe impairment) which includes significant impairment of intelligence and social functioning and is associated with abnormally aggressive or seriously irresponsible conduct...".

- *Psychopathic disorder*, which is "a persistent disorder or disability of mind (whether or not including significant impairment of intelligence) which results in abnormally aggressive or seriously irresponsible conduct ...".

(Mental Health Act 1983, Section 1(2) and 1(3))

## 3. Approved Social Workers

### 3.1 Duty of Local Authority

A local social services authority must appoint a sufficient number of approved social workers to undertake the functions conferred on them by the Act. Such social workers must undertake specialised training and have appropriate competence in dealing with persons who are suffering with mental disorder (Mental Health Act 1983, Section 114).

### 3.2 Duties of Approved Social Workers

3.2.1 It is the duty of an approved social worker (ASW)to make an application for admission to hospital (or a guardianship order) of a patient within his local authority area when relatives are unable or unwilling to do so, having taken into account the wishes expressed by relatives and any other relevant circumstances, and thinks it necessary or proper to make the application (Mental Health Act 1983, Section 13(1)).

3.2.2 The Code of Practice states that the ASW is usually the right applicant bearing in mind professional training, knowledge of legislation and of local resources together with the potential adverse effect that a nearest relative application might have on the relationship with the patient (7).

3.2.3 The ASW, before making an application, must interview the patient in a suitable manner and must satisfy himself that detention in hospital is, in all the circumstances of the case, the most appropriate way of providing the care and medical treatment the patient needs. The Code of Practice (8) gives detailed guidance on the manner of interview, including the use of interpreters (Mental Health Act 1983, Section 13(2)).

3.2.4 The ASW must take all practicable steps to inform the nearest relative (if any) that the application is about to be or has been made, and of the relative's powers to effect the discharge of the patient. The nearest relative has power to object to applications for admission for treatment or for reception into guardianship and if the relative objects the ASW cannot proceed with the application. However, if the ASW considers the objection unreasonable, he may apply to the county court for the function of the nearest relative to be performed by the applicant or other specified person suitable and willing to act as the nearest relative (Mental Health Act 1983, Section 11(3), 11(4) and 29(2)).

3.2.5 If required by the nearest relative, the social services authority shall direct an ASW, as soon as practicable, to take a patient's case into consideration with a view to making an application for his admission to hospital. If the ASW decides not to make an application, he must inform the nearest relative of his reasons in writing (Mental Health Act 1983, Section 13(4)).

3.2.6 Where a patient is admitted to hospital on application by his nearest relative (except under Section 4 for Emergency Admission for Assessment) a social worker – not necessarily an ASW – will be under a duty to provide a social circumstances report to the hospital managers (Mental Health Act 1983, Section 14).

3.2.7 The ASW also has a duty to interview patients removed to a Place of Safety by the police. See below. (Mental Health Act 1983, Section 136(2))

3.2.8 The duty of the local social services authority and district health authority to provide aftercare for certain patients, under Section 117, may also devolve to the ASW.

## 3.3 Powers of the Approved Social Worker

3.3.1 The ASW making the application has the authority to convey a patient to hospital or to authorise another in writing to do so. This authority expires 14 days after the medical examination or after 24 hours in the case of an emergency application. If necessary, it is the duty of the health authority to provide an ambulance. A similar authority is provided by Section 40(1) to convey to hospital a patient on whom a court has made a hospital order; this authority expires 28 days after the making of the order (Mental Health Act 1983, Section 6(1) and 40(1)).

3.3.2 An ASW, amongst others, has power to retake and return a patient absent without leave from hospital or guardianship. If, however, a detained patient remains absent without leave for 28 days, he cannot be retaken and his detention order lapses (Mental Health Act 1983, Section 18(1) and (4)).

3.3.3 For the purposes of taking into custody, or conveying or detaining a detained patient, an ASW has all the powers, authorities, protection and privileges which a constable has (Mental Health Act 1983, Section 137(2)).

3.3.4 An ASW may at all reasonable times after producing, if asked to do so, some duly authenticated document, enter and inspect any premises (not being a hospital) in the area of his local authority in which a mentally disordered patient is living, if he has reasonable cause to believe that the patient is not under proper care (Mental Health Act 1983, Section 115).

3.3.5 An ASW may apply to a magistrate for a warrant authorising any constable named in the warrant to enter,

if need be by force, any specified premises where there is
reasonable cause to suspect that a person believed to be
suffering from mental disorder

- has been, or is being, ill-treated, neglected or kept
otherwise than under proper control; or

- being unable to care for himself, is living alone.

The magistrate may issue a warrant enabling a constable
to enter the premises and, if necessary, remove the person
to a place of safety for assessment. The constable must be
accompanied by an approved social worker and a doctor.
The patient may be detained for up to seventy-two hours
(Mental Health Act 1983 Section 135(1)).

3.3.6 A similar process can apply when a detained patient has
absconded and there is reasonable cause to believe that the
patient is to be found on specified premises and admission
to the premises has been, or is likely to be, refused (Mental
Health Act 1983, Section 135(2)).

# 4. Informal Admission of Patients

## 4.1 Informal Admission as the Norm

4.1.1 The general principle is that people with problems of mental
health should have the same rights as any other patients
using a National Health Service facility. This is manifested
in Section 131 of the Act and in the Memorandum (9)
accompanying the Act published by the Department of
Health, which make it clear that, for anyone over the age
of sixteen years and capable of expressing his own wishes,
informal admission should be the norm "and should be
used whenever a patient is not unwilling to be admitted,
and can be treated without the use of compulsory powers".
Therefore, the patient does not have to express positive
willingness to enter hospital, as long as he is not unwilling.

4.1.2 The Code of Practice supports this norm, but goes on to
state that "compulsory admission should, however, be
considered where the patient's current mental state,

150

together with reliable evidence of past experience, indicates a strong likelihood that he will change his mind about informal admission prior to his actual admission to hospital with a resulting risk to his health and/or safety or to other persons". (10)

## 4.2 Rights of Informal Patients

4.2.1 Informal patients retain almost all their rights of citizenship, including the right to vote subject to their capacity to make a statutory declaration.

4.2.2 In particular they have the right to refuse treatment and to discharge themselves from the hospital.

## 4.3 Applications in respect of a Patient already in Hospital

4.3.1 When the legislation uses the terms 'admission' and 'discharge' in relation to compulsory powers, they relate to the patient entering or leaving a state of detention in hospital, not to the hospital premises. Thus, if in the case of a patient who is an inpatient in a hospital, it appears to the registered medical practitioner in charge of the treatment of the patient that an application ought to be made for the compulsory admission of the patient to the hospital, he may furnish a report in writing to that effect; and in any such case, the patient may be detained in the hospital for a period of 72 hours. (Mental Health Act 1983, Section 5(2)).

4.3.2 Similarly, if it appears to a nurse of the prescribed class that the patient is suffering from mental disorder to such a degree that it is necessary for his health or safety or for the protection of others for him to be immediately restrained from leaving the hospital and it is not practicable to secure the immediate attendance of a practitioner, the nurse may record that fact in writing and the patient may be detained for a period of not more than six hours. (Mental Health Act 1983, Section 5(4))

## 5. Compulsory Admission of Patients

### 5.1 Admission for Assessment

5.1.1 Application may be by an approved social worker or the nearest relative (Mental Health Act 1983, Section 11(1)).

5.1.2 The grounds are that the patient

- is suffering from mental disorder of a nature or degree which warrants the detention of the patient in a hospital for assessment (or for assessment followed by medical treatment) for at least a limited period; and

- ought to be so detained in the interests of his own health or safety or with a view to the protection of other persons (Mental Health Act 1983, Section 2(2)).

5.1.3 An application for admission for assessment shall be founded on the written recommendations in the prescribed forms of two registered medical practitioners (Mental Health Act 1983, Section 2(3)).

5.1.4 The patient may be detained for a period not exceeding twenty-eight days (Mental Health Act 1983, Section 2(4)).

5.1.5 The applicant must have personally seen the patient within the previous fourteen days; one of the doctors must be approved as having special experience in the diagnosis and treatment of mental disorder and one should, if practicable, have previous acquaintance with the patient. Admission must take place within fourteen days of the date of the second medical examination (Mental Health Act 1983, Section 11(5)).

5.1.6 The nearest relative cannot prevent an application under Section 2 if it is made by an ASW, but an order for discharge may be made by the responsible medical officer, by the hospital managers or by the nearest relative after giving seventy-two hours written notice and subject to bar by the responsible medical officer on the grounds that the patient would be likely to act in a manner dangerous to himself or others, or by a Mental Health Review Tribunal (Mental Health Act 1983, Sections 23(2) and 25(1)).

### 5.2 Admission for Assessment in Cases of Emergency

5.2.1 Application may be by an approved social worker or the nearest relative (Mental Health Act 1983, Section 4(2)).

5.2.2 The grounds are

- it is of urgent necessity for the patient to be admitted and detained under Section 2 above, and that compliance with the provisions of this part of the Act would involve undesirable delay (Mental Health Act 1983, Section 4(2)).

5.2.3 Therefore, an emergency application can be founded on one medical recommendation given, if practicable, by a practitioner who has previous acquaintance with the patient. The doctor need not be approved (Mental Health Act 1983, Section 4(3)).

5.2.4 The applicant must have seen the patient within the previous twenty-four hours of the application being made (Mental Health Act 1983, Section 4(5)).

5.2.5 An emergency application shall cease to have effect on the expiration of a period of seventy-two hours from the time when the patient is admitted to the hospital, unless the second medical recommendation required by Section 2 above is given and received by the managers within that period (Mental Health Act 1983, Section 4(4)).

5.2.6 There is no power to impose treatment.

5.2.7 There is no formal power of discharge or appeal to a Mental Health Review Tribunal in respect of emergency admissions for assessment.

### 5.3 Admission for treatment

5.3.1 Application may be by an approved social worker or the nearest relative (Mental Health Act 1983 Section 11(1)).

5.3.2 The grounds are that the patient

- is suffering from mental illness, severe mental impairment, psychopathic disorder or mental impairment and his mental disorder is of a nature or degree which makes

153

it appropriate for him to receive medical treatment in a hospital; and

- in the case of psychopathic disorder or mental impairment, such treatment is likely to alleviate or prevent a deterioration of his condition; and

- it is necessary for the health or safety of the patient or for the protection of other persons that he should receive such treatment, and it cannot be provided unless he is detained under this section (Mental Health Act 1983, Section 3(2)).

5.3.3 Such an application shall not be made by an approved social worker if the nearest relative objects, and no such application shall be made except after consultation with the nearest relative unless it appears to the social worker that such consultation is not reasonably practicable or would involve unreasonable delay (Mental Health Act 1983, Section 11(4)).

5.3.4 An application for admission for treatment shall be founded on the written recommendations in the prescribed forms of two registered medical practitioners (Mental Health Act 1983, Section 3(3)).

5.3.5 The patient may be detained for a period not exceeding six months unless authority for his detention is renewed, for a further period of six months, then for a further period of one year and so on for periods of one year at a time (Mental Health Act 1983, Section 20(1) and (2)).

5.3.6 The applicant must have personally seen the patient within the fourteen days preceding the application; one of the doctors must be approved as having special experience in the diagnosis and treatment of mental disorder, and one should, if practicable, have previous acquaintance with the patient. Both medical recommendations must specify at least one form of mental disorder in common. Admission must take place within fourteen days of the date of the later medical examination (Mental Health Act 1983, Section 11(5)).

5.3.7 An order for discharge may be made by the responsible medical officer, by the hospital managers, or by the nearest relative after giving seventy-two hours written notice and subject to bar by the responsible medical officer on the grounds of danger (Mental Health Act 1983, Sections 23(2) and 25(1)).

5.3.8 A patient detained under Section 3 may also be discharged by a Mental Health Review Tribunal if he applies within the first six months of detention, then once during each period of renewal. The nearest relative may apply to the tribunal if his order for discharge has been barred under Section 25(1) on the grounds that the patient would be likely to act in a manner dangerous to other persons or to himself (Mental Health Act 1983, Section 66(1) and (2) and Section 72(1)).

## 6. Guardianship

### 6.1 The Nature of Guardianship

6.1.1 Treatment in the community is preferable to admission to hospital, but in some instances some power to direct the patient's life may be necessary, and this is where guardianship comes in.

6.1.2 Guardianship orders may be made under Part II of the 1983 Act – which covers compulsory admission to hospital and guardianship – or under Part III of the Act – which relates to patients concerned in criminal proceedings. The law in respect of criminal proceedings is considered in the next chapter of this book.

6.1.3 Application under Part II may be made by an approved social worker or the nearest relative (Mental Health Act 1983, Section 11(1)).

### 6.2 Admission into Guardianship

6.2.1 An application may be made in respect of a patient who has attained the age of sixteen years, for him to be received into the guardianship of either a social services department or a named person on whose behalf guardianship has been accepted by his local social services department (Mental Health Act 1983, Section 7(1) and (5)).

6.2.2 The grounds are that the patient

- is suffering from mental disorder, being mental illness, severe mental impairment, psychopathic disorder or mental impairment and his mental disorder is of a nature or degree which warrants his reception into guardianship; and

- it is necessary in the interests of the welfare of the patient or for the protection of other persons that the patient should be so received.

(Mental Health Act 1983, Section 7(2))

6.2.3 A guardianship application shall be founded on the written recommendations in the prescribed forms of two registered medical practitioners (Mental Health Act 1983, Section 7(3)).

6.2.4 The patient may be kept under guardianship for a period not exceeding six months unless the authority for his guardianship is renewed, for a further period of six months, then for a further period of one year and so on for periods of one year at a time (Mental Health Act 1983, Section 20(1) and (2)).

6.2.5 The applicant must have personally seen the patient within the previous fourteen days; one of the doctors must be approved as having special experience in the diagnosis and treatment of mental disorder and one should, if practicable, have previous acquaintance with the patient (Mental Health Act 1983 Section 11(5) and 12(2)).

6.2.6 The guardianship order confers on the social services department or the named person

- the power to require the patient to reside at a place specified by them

- the power to require the patient to attend at places and times so specified for mental treatment, occupation, education or training

- the power to require access to the patient to be given at any place where the patient is residing, to any registered medical practitioner, approved social worker or other person so specified (Mental Health Act 1983, Section 8(1)).

6.2.7 Guardianship does not restrict a patient's access to hospital services on a voluntary basis, and the order can remain in force if the patient is admitted under Sections 2 and 4, but it does not remain in force if the patient is admitted for treatment under Section 3.

## 6.3 Duties of Guardians

6.3.1 Private guardians have the following duties:

- to appoint a registered medical practitioner to act as the nominated medical attendant of the patient

- to notify the responsible local social services authority of the name and address of the nominated medical attendant

- to comply with such directions as that authority may give

- to furnish that authority with all such reports or other information with regard to the patient as the authority may from time to time require

- to notify that authority

  - on the reception of that patient into guardianship, of his address and the address of the patient

  - of any permanent change of either address, before or not later than 7 days after the change takes place

- where on any permanent change of his address, the new address is in the area of a different local social services authority, to notify that authority

  - of his address and that of the patient

  - of the name and address of the nominated medical attendant and to send a copy of the notification to the authority which was formerly responsible.

- in the event of the death of the patient or the termination of the guardianship by discharge, transfer or otherwise, to notify the responsible social services authority as soon as reasonably practicable.

(Mental Health (Hospital, Guardianship and Consent to Treatment) Regulations 1983, Regulation 12)

6.3.2 The responsible social services authority must

- arrange for every patient received into guardianship under Part II of the Act to be visited at such intervals as the authority may decide, but in any case, at intervals of not more than 3 months, and at least one such visit in any year shall be by a practitioner approved by the Secretary of State (Mental Health (Hospital, Guardianship and Consent to Treatment) Regulations 1983, Regulation 13).

6.3.3 The Code of Practice (11) sets out the components of effective guardianship and points out that, where it is used, it must be part of the patient's overall care and treatment plan.

6.3.4 Sections 127 to 130 of the 1983 Act establish offences and set out penalties for a guardian who ill-treats, or wilfully neglects a patient, assists a patient to be absent without leave, or obstructs an authorised person to visit, examine or interview a patient. The local authority may prosecute with the consent of the Director of Public Prosecutions.

## 6.4 Discharge of Guardianship

6.4.1 An order for the discharge of guardianship can be made by the responsible local social services authority or by the nearest relative (Mental Health Act 1983, Section 23(2)).

6.4.2 Discharge by the nearest relative cannot be barred, subject to the displacement of the nearest relative by a court under Section 29, and is effective when the local social services authority receives the order for discharge.

6.4.3 A patient may also be discharged by a Mental Health Review Tribunal if he applies within six months of the guardianship order being made, then once during each period of renewal (Mental Health Act 1983, Section 66(1) and (2) and Section 72(4)).

## 7. Care and Control of Persons Found in a Public Place

### 7.1 Police Powers

7.1.1 If a constable finds in a public place a person who appears to him to be suffering from mental disorder and to be in immediate need of care or control, the constable may, if he thinks it necessary to do so in the interests of that person or for the protection of other persons, remove that person to a place of safety (Mental Health Act 1983, Section 136(1)).

7.1.2 A person removed to a place of safety under this section may be detained there for a period not exceeding 72 hours for the purpose of enabling him to be examined by a registered medical practitioner and to be interviewed by an approved social worker and of making any necessary arrangements for his treatment or care (Mental Health Act 1983, Section 136(2)).

### 7.2 Information about Rights

7.2.1 Where an individual has been arrested by the police under Section 136

- he is entitled to have another person of his choice informed of his arrest and whereabouts

- he has a right of access to legal advice if he is in police detention (i.e. a police station is being used as a place of safety)

- access to legal advice should be facilitated if requested where detention is in a place of safety other than a police station (Police and Criminal Evidence Act 1984 Section 56 and Section 58).

7.2.2 Where a hospital is used as a place of safety, the managers must ensure that the provisions of Section 132 of the Mental Health Act 1983 regarding information to be given to detained patients are complied with (see below).

7.2.3 The Code of Practice (12) recommends that the same information as for Section 132 should be given when a police station is a place of safety, although Section 132 does not apply.

## 7.3 Treatment

7.3.1 Part IV of the Mental Health Act 1983, which relates to consent to treatment, does not apply to persons detained under Section 136; hence the person can only be treated in the absence of consent in accordance with common law.

7.3.2 Of course, applications for compulsory admission under Sections 2 or 3 of the Mental Health Act 1983 may be made while the person is detained under Section 136.

# 8. Treatment and Care of Patients

## 8.1 The Rights of Detained Patients

8.1.1 The hospital managers are required to inform a detained patient, both verbally and in writing, of the following

- under which provision of the Mental Health Act 1983 he is being detained and the effects of that provision

- his rights to apply to a Mental Health Review Tribunal

- his rights regarding consent to treatment

- his right to receive post, and the limitations on this.

The managers are required to ensure that the patient understands these rights as far as practicable (Mental Health Act 1983, Section 132).

8.1.2 If the patient is detained under Sections 4, 5, 135 or 136 (or Sections 35 or 37(4) in criminal proceedings) he has the same right to refuse treatment as an informal patient.

160

8.1.3 If the patient is detained under other Sections of the 1983 Act he has the right to refuse consent

- to treatment which requires both his consent and a second medical opinion, namely, any surgical operation for destroying brain tissue or for destroying the functioning of brain tissue, or the surgical implantation of hormones for the purpose of reducing male sexual drive

- to treatment which requires either his consent or the support of a second medical opinion, namely ECT or medication continued 3 months after it was first administered. If the patient refuses consent, the treatment may still be given if a second medical opinion agrees that it should be given (Mental Health Act 1983, Section 57 and Section 58).

8.1.4 Other medical treatment for his mental disorder cannot be refused provided it is prescribed by the responsible medical officer, but the patient retains the right to withdraw consent to any of the treatments requiring his consent even when it has begun. In that event treatment must cease until consent is obtained or, where applicable, overridden by a second medical opinion (Mental Health Act 1983, Section 60 and Section 63).

8.1.5 Consent is not required for an urgent treatment which is necessary to save a patient's life (Mental Health Act 1983, Section 62).

## 8.2 The Right of All Patients to Protection against Ill-treatment or Sexual Exploitation

8.2.1 It is an offence for any staff member of a hospital or nursing home to ill-treat or wilfully neglect an inpatient or outpatient (Mental Health Act 1983, Section 127(1)).

8.2.2 Under Section 128 of the Mental Health Act 1959, which was not repealed by the 1983 Act, but as amended by the Sexual Offences Act 1967, it is an offence for a man who is employed in a hospital or nursing home, or who is the guardian of a patient, or who has care or custody of the

161

patient, to have sexual intercourse with a woman patient or commit homosexual acts with a male patient.

## 8.3 The Rights of the Nearest Relative

8.3.1 Relatives are defined as

- husband or wife (including cohabitees of more than six months cohabitation)
- son or daughter
- father or mother
- brother or sister
- grandparent
- grandchild
- uncle or aunt
- niece or nephew

and the 'nearest relative' is the person first described in this list, with the elder or eldest in any category taking precedence, regardless of sex (Mental Health Act 1983, Section 26).

8.3.2 At different points throughout this chapter, reference has been made to the following rights of the nearest relative

- the right to require a local authority to assess a patient
- the right to make applications
- the right to be informed of applications made or to be made by an approved social worker
- the right to be consulted about, and the right to block, applications for treatment or for guardianship
- rights to order the discharge of patients detained under Section 2 or 3 or received into guardianship under Section 7
- rights to apply to a Mental Health Review Tribunal.

8.3.3 In addition, nearest relatives have the following rights

- the right to arrange for any registered medical practitioner to visit the patient and examine him in private, when he is considering applying for discharge of a patient detained in hospital or under guardianship

• the right to be informed, if the patient agrees, of the patient's discharge, if practicable at least 7 days before the date of discharge (Mental Health Act 1983 Section 24(1) and Section 133(1) and (2)).

## 8.4 Code of Practice

The Code of Practice (12) sets out in considerable detail the practice to be followed in respect of the treatment and care of patients in hospital, including

• medical treatment and second opinions

• patients presenting particular management problems

• psychological treatments

• leave of absence and absence without leave

• the review of detention

• personal searches

## 8.5 Complaints

The Hospital Complaints Procedures Act 1985 places a duty upon health authorities to investigate any complaint on the part of a patient about any aspect of his treatment. The Department of Health and Welsh Office Circulars HC(88)37 and WHC(88) 36 respectively, issued in June 1988, set out both the duties and procedures for making complaints and for their investigation.

## 8.6 Mental Health Act Commission

A Mental Health Act Commission has been set up which includes amongst its functions

• visiting and interviewing patients

• investigating complaints by patients and non-patients

• investigating complaints by Members of Parliament

• reviewing informal patients

• reporting to Parliament

(Mental Health Act, 1983 Section 121)

# 9. Aftercare

## 9.1 The Statutory Basis of Aftercare

9.1.1 It is the duty of the district health authority and the social services authority to provide, in co-operation with relevant voluntary agencies, aftercare services for patients who have been detained for treatment (Section 3 of the 1983 Act) or under a hospital order (Section 37) or those in hospital following a transfer direction (Sections 47 and 48), until such time as the authorities are satisfied that the person concerned is no longer in need of such services (Mental Health Act 1983, Section 117).

9.1.2 Services provided under Section 117 are 'community care services' within the meaning of the National Health Service and Community Care Act 1990 and must, therefore, be included in local authorities' community care plans (National Health Service and Community Care Act 1990, Section 46(3)).

## 9.2 The Code of Practice

9.2.1 The Code of Practice (14) states that the purpose of aftercare is to enable a patient to return to his home or accommodation other than a hospital or nursing home, and to minimise the chances of him needing any future in-patient hospital care.

9.2.2 When a decision has been taken to discharge or grant leave to a patient, it is the responsibility of the responsible medical officer to ensure that a discussion takes place to establish a care plan to organise the management of the patient's continuing health and social care needs. Included in the discussion should be

- the patient's responsible medical officer
- a nurse involved in caring for the patient in hospital
- a social worker specialising in mental health work
- the GP
- a community psychiatric nurse

- a representative of relevant voluntary organisations

- the patient if he wishes and/or a relative or other nominated representative (15).

9.2.3 The discussion should include the appointment of a key worker from one of the statutory agencies to monitor the care plan's implementation, liaise and co-ordinate where necessary and report to the senior officer in their agency any problems that arise which cannot be resolved through normal discussion. It will also be the responsibility of the key worker to arrange regular reviews of the plan until it is agreed that it is no longer necessary (16).

## 10. Court of Protection and Enduring Powers of Attorney

### 10.1 The Court of Protection

10.1.1 The Court of Protection is an office of the Supreme Court. Its function is to manage and administer the property and affairs of people who, through mental disorder, are incapable of managing their own financial affairs. The Court draws its powers from the Mental Health Act 1983 and the Court of Protection Rules 1984. Anyone who considers that the affairs and property of someone else may require the protection of the Court can ask for its help.

10.1.2 The Protection Division of the Public Trust Office carries out the administrative functions on behalf of the Court of Protection, and is the normal point of contact. Its address is The Public Trust Office, Protection Division, Stewart House, 24 Kingsway, London, WC2B 6JX. If guidance is needed urgently the Enquiries Branch can be contacted on 071 269 7000 extensions 7358, 7157, 7446, 7074, 7235 or 7126.

10.1.3 The court has wide powers in respect of a patient's financial affairs, including appointing someone to act on behalf of a patient. Such a person is called a 'receiver', and is often a relative or close friend, or sometimes an officer of a local authority. The order appointing a Receiver gives details of the specific powers conferred on the Receiver, which are usually quite limited. Additional orders or authorities may be issued by the Court from time to time varying or extending the Receiver's powers.

10.1.4 The Receivership will come to an end

- on the Court being satisfied that the patient has recovered and is once again able to manage his own affairs; or

- if the Receiver wishes to retire or if for some other reason it becomes necessary to appoint a new Receiver; or

- on the patient's death.

## 10.2 Enduring Powers of Attorney

10.2.1 A power of attorney is a formal instrument by which one person authorises another to perform certain acts for him. An ordinary power of attorney loses its validity when the person creating it loses the mental capacity to manage his or her own affairs. An enduring power of attorney is a power of attorney which, subject to conditions and safeguards, continues in force even after the maker of the power (called 'the donor') becomes mentally incapable of handling his or her own affairs, provided that it is registered.

10.2.2 An enduring power of attorney made after 31 July 1991 must be in the exact form prescribed by the Enduring Powers of Attorney (Prescribed Form) Regulations 1990. A form can be purchased from legal stationers, or one may be prepared by a solicitor or by the donor provided it is in the form set out in the Regulations. The attorney must be at least eighteen, mentally capable and not bankrupt.

10.2.3. An enduring power of attorney may give a general authority, a specific authority or a general or specific authority with restrictions and conditions. The donor must be mentally capable of understanding what an enduring power is and what it is intended to do, and someone (not one of the attorneys) must witness the donor's signature by being present when the donor signs the power.

10.2.4 When the attorney believes that the donor is or is becoming mentally incapable, the attorney must apply to register the enduring power of attorney with the Court of Protection before he can get or continue to act under it. The address is given above in paragraph 10.1.2.

10.2.5 When the enduring power of attorney has been registered, the attorney, even if given authority without any restrictions or conditions, must act reasonably and have regard to the limits imposed by the Enduring Powers of Attorney Act 1985. An explanatory booklet can be obtained from the Public Trust Office.

## References

1. Olsen, M. Rolf (Ed)(1984) "Social Work and Mental Health", Tavistock, London.

2. DHSS (1971) "Better Services for the Mentally Handicapped", HMSO Cmnd 4683, London.

3. DHSS (1975) "Better Services for the Mentally Ill", HMSO Cmnd 6233, London.

4. DHSS (1976) "A Review of the Mental Health Act 1959", HMSO, London.

5. DHSS (1981) "Care in the Community", HMSO, London.

6. DHSS (1989) "Caring for People", HMSO, Cmnd 849, London, paragraph 7.5

7. Department of Health and Welsh Office (1990) "Code of Practice - Mental Health Act 1983", HMSO, London, paragraph 2.30

8. Department of Health and Welsh Office (1990) "Code of Practice - Mental Health Act 1983", HMSO, London, paragraphs 2.10, 2.11 and 2.12.

9. Department of Health (1987) "Mental Health Act 1983", Memorandum on Parts I to VI, VIII and X, HMSO, London.

10. Department of Health and Welsh Office (1990) "Code of Practice - Mental Health Act 1983", HMSO, London, paragraph 2.7

11. Department of Health and Welsh Office (1990) "Code of Practice - Mental Health Act 1983", HMSO, London, paragraph 13.1 to 13.9.

12. Department of Health and Welsh Office (1990) "Code of Practice - Mental Health Act 1983", HMSO, London, paragraph 10.11.

13. Department of Health and Welsh Office (1990) "Code of Practice - Mental Health Act 1983", HMSO, London.

14. Department of Health and Welsh Office (1990) "Code of Practice - Mental Health Act 1983", HMSO, London, paragraph 26.1

15. Department of Health and Welsh Office (1990) "Code of Practice - Mental Health Act 1983", HMSO, London, paragraph 26.6 and 26.7.

16. Department of Health and Welsh Office (1990) "Code of Practice - Mental Health Act 1983", HMSO, London, paragraph 26.9 and 26.11.

## Chapter Four

# The Care and Control of Offenders in the Community

## Introduction

Offenders it seems, like the poor, are always with us. The statute book shows a legislative litany of this society's attempts to respond to offenders and their behaviour. There have been five Criminal Justice Acts since 1972 and the latest – the Criminal Justice Act 1991 – is the third in less than ten years.

The tempo of its entry into our law was swift. A White Paper (1), published in February 1990, proposed significant changes in the powers of the courts to deal with offenders, and this was quickly followed by a Green Paper entitled 'Supervision and Punishment in the Community' (2) on the organisation of the Probation Service and how community penalties should be put into effect. The Bill was introduced in November 1990, the Act received the Royal Assent in July 1991, some provisions came into force in October 1991, and those on sentencing are to be implemented from October 1992. This chapter has been written as though the Criminal Justice Act 1991 were in operation.

Rigorous criminological analyses abound, but put simply the trends, such as they are, of the legislation during the twentieth century could be said to be as follows:

- Young offenders came slowly to be treated as different from adult offenders, and needing special considerations; but as the century closes, 'youth' remains as disconcerting as ever, and a potentially confusing flexible jurisdiction relates to those under the age of twenty-one.

- A primary concern of the second half of the century has been how to contain adult offenders, while increasingly aware of how much it costs society to do so; without too directly confronting judicial freedom, a series of Criminal Justice Acts has sought to offer and require consideration of community-based penalties for certain categories of offenders and to emphasise 'proportionality' in sentencing.

- Mentally disordered offenders have, with this century's developments in psychiatry, come to be seen as a group apart, needing particular provision; but as the final decade has begun, awareness has heightened that despite their special needs they continue to form a substantial proportion of the prison population.

While the emphasis, therefore, is on control, there are strands of care running through the law in respect of offenders. The tension between care and control is particularly acute in respect of young offenders. Containment in the community of those adults who have not committed serious, violent or sexual offences has become a new imperative, given the economic and social costs of high levels of imprisonment. The cautious care and control of mentally disordered offenders in either the community or in compulsory detention has become the hallmark of the approach to this group. Being provided with 'aftercare', or being licensed or 'paroled' back into the community is a feature common to young offenders, adult offenders and mentally disordered offenders. It is as three interlocking groups that this chapter seeks to set out the law on the care and control of offenders in the community.

## 1. Young Offenders

### 1.1 Prevention of Crime and Diversion from Prosecution

1.1.1 Every local authority must take reasonable steps

- to encourage juveniles within its area not to commit offences

- to reduce the need to bring criminal proceedings against juveniles.

(Children Act 1989, Schedule 2, Paragraph 7)

1.1.2 The Department of Health's guidance on the Children Act (3) states that the services which local authorities can make available include

- the provision of advice and support to parents, given the role of parents in discouraging offending

- 'preventative' intermediate treatment for young people at risk of offending

170

- supervision for juvenile offenders (where authorised by a court), with or without intensive intermediate treatment

- the general provision of youth and community services.

1.1.3 The guidance (4) indicates that the local authorities will need to review the range of facilities, collect data on the patterns of juvenile offending and on the gender and ethnicity of juvenile offenders and to monitor the local juvenile justice system.

1.1.4 Local authorities have been recommended to establish a standing committee, representing relevant agencies, to formulate and keep under review a strategy for crime prevention, in general, and the circular (Inter-departmental Circular LAC(90)5 'Crime Prevention – the Success of the Partnership Approach') includes advice on juvenile crime prevention.

1.1.5 Home Office Circular 59/1990, 'The Cautioning of Offenders', stresses the importance of inter-agency participation in relation to the cautioning of offenders, and advises that in making individual decisions about juveniles the police should invite juvenile liaison panels to review any case where the decision whether or not to caution a juvenile is in doubt.

## 1.2 Meaning of Young Offender

1.2.1 The age of criminal responsibility is ten years; below that age a child cannot commit a crime and so cannot be subjected to criminal proceedings (Children and Young Persons Act 1933, Section 50, as amended).

1.2.2 A child aged ten years but under fourteen years cannot be convicted of an offence unless it is first proved to the court that he knew what he was doing was wrong. The court starts with the 'evidential presumption' (i.e. a presumption in the absence of evidence to the contrary) that such a child did not know what it was doing was wrong.

1.2.3 A young person aged fourteen years to sixteen years is presumed to have full capacity to commit a crime. The term 'young person' has for some time applied to this age group. However, the Criminal Justice Act 1991 has introduced provision whereby persons aged seventeen years are to be treated as young persons for certain purposes. The effect of this change is that those up to the age of eighteen will now be treated, in general, as young offenders in respect of the following enactments

- the Children and Young Persons Acts 1933 to 1969

- the Prison Act 1952, Section 43(3) – which relates to remand centres, young offender institutions, etc.

- the Rehabilitation of Offenders Act 1974 – which provides for rehabilitation periods to be reduced by half for young offenders.

(Criminal Justice Act 1991, Section 68 and Schedule 8)

1.2.4　Juvenile courts are renamed as youth courts and will now hear criminal cases in respect of those aged ten to seventeen years. The adult courts will relate to those aged eighteen and over. Young people aged seventeen will, however, continue to be treated as adults for pre-trial purposes (Criminal Justice Act 1991 Section 70(1)).

1.2.5　Despite appearing in the adult court, the young person is a young offender until reaching the age of twenty-one, and special limitations apply in respect of custodial sentences imposed upon them. See below paragraph 1.6.12.

1.3　**The Detention, Treatment and Questioning of Juveniles by Police Officers.**

1.3.1　The law in respect of police powers when detaining or questioning persons is substantially contained in the Police and Criminal Evidence Act 1984. The Act is accompanied by Codes of Practice (5), which provide detailed guidelines for the operation of the Act.

1.3.2　The Code of Practice for the Detention, Treatment and Questioning of Persons by Police Officers – Code C – while relating to all persons, includes special provisions in respect of juveniles.

1.3.3 The Code states that a juvenile must not be interviewed or asked to provide or sign a written statement in the absence of an 'appropriate adult' unless an officer of the rank of superintendent or above considers that delay will involve an immediate risk of harm to persons or serious loss of or serious damage to property (6). An appropriate adult could be a parent, guardian or, if in care, a representative of the care authority, or a social worker or other responsible adult who is not a police officer (7).

1.3.4 The Code of Practice makes it clear that the purpose of the appropriate adult's attendance is not merely to act as an observer but to advise the person being questioned and to observe whether or not the interview is being conducted properly and fairly, and to facilitate communication with the person being interviewed (8).

1.3.5 A juvenile who has been arrested and detained must be moved to local authority accommodation while awaiting appearance in court except in the following limited circumstances:

- the custody officer certifies that it is impracticable, or

- in the case of an arrested juvenile who has attained the age of fifteen years, the custody officer certifies that no secure accommodation is available and that keeping him in other local authority accommodation would be inadequate to protect the public from serious harm from him.

(Police and Criminal Evidence Act 1984, Section 38 as amended by Criminal Justice Act 1991, Section 59)

## 1.4 Juvenile Remands

1.4.1 Sections 60 to 62 of the Criminal Justice Act 1991 make provision for the eventual abolition of the practice of remanding fifteen and sixteen-year-old males to prison department establishments. Under interim arrangements, the option of penal remand will remain available to courts if:

- he is charged with or has been convicted of a violent or sexual offence, or an offence punishable in the case of an adult with imprisonment for fourteen years or more; or

- he has a recent history of absconding while remanded to local authority accommodation, and is charged with or has been convicted of an imprisonable offence alleged or found to have been committed while he was so remanded

and (in either case) the court is of opinion that only remanding him to a remand centre or prison would be adequate to protect the public from serious harm from him (Criminal Justice Act 1991, Section 62, amending the Children and Young Persons Act 1969, Section 23).

1.4.2 Under Section 60, a court remanding a person to local authority accommodation has a new power, after consultation with the local authority, to require the person to comply with any conditions as could be imposed under Section 3(6) of the Bail Act 1976 if he were then being granted bail (Criminal Justice Act 1991, Section 60(7), amending the Children and Young Persons Act 1969, Section 23).

1.4.3 In the longer term, once there is general agreement that adequate alternative arrangements exist, juvenile penal remands will be abolished (9).

## 1.5 Young Offenders in Court

1.5.1 Since the Children and Young Persons Act 1933 there has been provision relating to the attendance of parents or guardians at court hearings in respect of juveniles. The Criminal Justice Act 1991 amends that provision, making a clear distinction between 10-15 year-olds and 16-17 year-olds. In respect of the younger age group, the court must require the parent or guardian to attend during all stages of the proceedings unless it is unreasonable to do so. In respect of the older age group, the court may require such attendance. Where a local authority has parental responsibility for the child, the requirement to attend court falls on that authority (Criminal Justice Act 1991, Section 56).

174

1.5.2 The procedures in the Youth Court are essentially the same as in the adult magistrates' court, but they are conducted in a less formal way and usually in a less forbidding courtroom. In a trial, a simpler form of oath is also used.

1.5.3 Members of the public are not allowed to be present in youth courts unless they are directly involved in the case. The press may attend but they are not allowed to publish any details that might lead to the identification of the child, unless the court or the Home Secretary expressly dispenses with this requirement in the interests of justice. This restriction relates to the court not to young offenders *per se*, and therefore does not necessarily apply when young people appear in other courts.

1.5.4 A young offender may appear in an adult court when jointly charged or is in some other way connected with a person aged 18 or over, but there is provision for a magistrates' court to remit a person under 18 to the youth court for trial, in certain circumstances, or for an order to be made which only the youth court has power to make.

1.5.5 If a child or young person is charged with an offence which, in the case of an adult, is punishable on indictment with 14 years imprisonment or more, a youth court may commit him for trial in the Crown Court. In the event of a child being charged with homicide, the case is only triable on indictment at the Crown Court, but committal takes place in a youth court.

1.5.6 It is the duty of the local authority, unless they are of opinion that it is unnecessary to do so, to make such investigations and provide the court before which the proceedings are heard with such information relating to the home surroundings, school records, health and character of the person in respect of whom the proceedings are brought as appear to the authority likely to assist the court (Children and Young Persons Act 1969, Section 9(1)).

1.5.7 There is provision for local arrangements to be made for reports on home surroundings to be provided by a

175

probation officer (Children and Young Persons Act 1969, Section 34(3)).

1.5.8 The court must arrange for copies of any written report to be made available to legal representatives and parents. The report should also be made available to the young offender unless the court directs otherwise on the grounds of his age, understanding or possibility of suffering serious harm (Magistrates' Courts (Children and Young Persons) Rules 1988, Rule 10(2)).

## 1.6 Sentencing Options in the Youth Court

### 1.6.1 Deferment of Sentence

- The court may defer passing sentence on an offender for the purpose of enabling it to have regard, in determining his sentence, to his conduct after conviction (including, where appropriate, the making of reparation for his offence) or to any changes in his circumstances. The deferment (once only) must be to a date specified not more than six months after the date of conviction. The offender must consent (Powers of the Criminal Courts Act 1973, Section 1).

### 1.6.2 Bind Over

- The parent or guardian of a young offender aged under 16 must be bound over if the court is satisfied that to do so would be desirable in the interests of preventing the commission by the young person of further offences. If the court is not so satisfied, it must state so in open court and give reasons for that view (Criminal Justice Act 1991, Section 58(1)).

- The binding over of a minor's parent or guardian requires their consent, can be in a sum not exceeding £1,000, and is "to take proper care of him and exercise proper control over him" (Criminal Justice Act 1991, Section 58(2)).

- If the parent or guardian refuses consent and the court considers the refusal unreasonable, the court may order the parent or guardian to pay a fine not exceeding £1,000 (Criminal Justice Act 1991, Section 58(2)).

- The duration of the recognisance is until the offender reaches the age of 18 years, or for three years, whichever is the shorter (Criminal Justice Act 1991, Section 58(3)).

- The court may order forfeiture of the whole or part of the recognisance, and forfeiture would normally be triggered by the commission of a further offence.

- There is a right of appeal against such a binding over, to the Crown Court from the magistrates' court and to the Court of Appeal from the Crown Court (Criminal Justice Act 1991, Section 58(6) and (7)).

- The court may vary or revoke the bind over if, on application of the parent or guardian, it appears to the court, having regard to any change in the circumstances since the order was made to be in the interests of justice to do so (Criminal Justice Act 1991, Section 58(8)).

### 1.6.3 Absolute Discharge or Conditional Discharge

- An absolute discharge, or discharge subject to the condition that the offender commits no offence during a specified period not exceeding three years, can be made for an offence for which the sentence is not fixed by law (Powers of the Criminal Court Act 1973, Section 7).

### 1.6.4 Fine

- The Crown Court can impose the same level of fine on a young offender as on an adult.

- The youth court can impose a fine up to a maximum of £250 on a child (i.e. ten to thirteen year-olds) and up to a maximum of £1,000 on a young person (i.e. fourteen to seventeen year-olds) (Criminal Justice Act 1991, Section 17(2)).

- Although the fine is imposed on the young offender, the court orders the parent or guardian to pay it; but for offenders aged sixteen to seventeen, the former duty of the court to make an order requiring parents to pay has become a power to make such an order (Children and Young Persons Act 1933, Section 55, as amended by Criminal Justice Act 1991, Section 57(1)).

- fines will be fixed by 'units' (see below paragraph 2.5.4) and the court must allow the parent or guardian, if present, to make representations as to whether a fine should be imposed and the level of any fine, and take into account the parents' means (Criminal Justice Act 1991, Section 57(3)).

- local authorities can be ordered to pay fines in respect of children for whom they have parental responsibility, and will be deemed to have the maximum means when the level of fine is calculated (Criminal Justice Act 1991, Section 57(2) and (4)).

### 1.6.5 Supervision Order

- A supervision order can be imposed on a young offender aged ten to seventeen years of age (Children and Young Persons Act 1969, Section 7(7), as amended by Criminal Justice Act 1991, Section 68)

- An order can be for up to three years (hence it can continue after the supervisee reaches 18)

- The order places the young offender under the supervision of a local authority or a probation officer, and the supervisor has a duty to advise, assist and befriend the young offender (Children and Young Persons Act 1969, Sections 11, 13 and 14)

- The supervised person is required

  - to inform the supervisor at once of any change in his residence or employment

  - to keep in touch with the supervisor in accordance with such instructions as may from time to time be given by the supervisor and, in particular, if the supervisor so requires, receive visits from the supervisor at his home

  - to be of good behaviour

(Children and Young Persons Act 1969, Section 7(7) and Magistrates' Courts (Children and Young Persons) Rules 1988)

- The supervision order may also require the supervised person to comply with any directions given by the supervisor requiring him
  - to live at a place or places specified in the directions for a period or periods specified
  - to present himself to a person or persons specified in the directions at a place or places and on a day or days so specified
  - to participate in activities specified in the directions on a day or days so specified

  but it shall be for the supervisor to decide whether and to what extent he exercises power to give directions, but the total number of days a person may be required to comply with such directions shall not exceed 90 or such lesser number as specified in the order (Children and Young Persons Act 1969, Section 12, as amended by Criminal Justice Act 1982, Section 20)

- The court may go beyond giving discretionary authority to the supervisor to itself stipulating requirements to be carried out as part of a supervision order, if it has first consulted the supervisor and the supervised person (or if he is a child, his parent or guardian) consents, the requirements can then be
  - to do anything that the supervisor – as above – would have power to direct him to do
  - to remain for specified periods between 6pm and 6am at a place or places specified in the order
  - to refrain from participating in activities specified in the order

  but the total number of days for such stipulated intermediate treatment requirements shall not exceed 90, and a night restriction shall not be imposed in respect of any day outside the first three months of the order, and shall not be for more than 30 days in all (Children and Young Persons Act 1969, Section 12, as amended by Criminal Justice Act 1982, Section 20).

- Where a court is satisfied, on the evidence of an approved medical practitioner, that the mental condition of a supervised person is such as requires and may be susceptible to treatment but is not such as to warrant a hospital order, it may include in the supervision order a requirement that the supervised person submit to treatment, but if the person concerned has attained the age of fourteen he must consent to the inclusion of such a condition, and the requirement shall not in any case continue in force after the supervised person becomes eighteen. Where a requirement of medical treatment conflicts with a residence requirement or an intermediate treatment requirement, the medical requirement takes precedence (Children and Young Persons Act 1969, Section 12B).

- A supervision order may require a supervised person, if he is of compulsory school age, to comply with such arrangements for his education as may from time to time be made by his parent, the court having first consulted the supervisor and the local education authority (Children and Young Persons Act 1969, Section 12C, as amended by Criminal Justice Act 1988, Schedule 10).

- A supervision order may include a residence requirement requiring the juvenile to live for a specified period not exceeding six months in local authority accommodation, if all the following conditions are satisfied:

  - a criminal supervision order has previously been made in respect of the juvenile which included either a requirement to take part in a programme of intermediate treatment or a residence requirement

  - he is found guilty of an offence which was committed while the previous order was in force is an imprisonable offence if committed by a person over twenty-one, and in the opinion of the court is serious

  - the court is satisfied that the behaviour was due to a significant extent, to the circumstances in which he was living

180

and the court must obtain a pre-sentence report and consult with the local authority and the juvenile must be legally represented or have refused the offer of legal aid or have been refused it because of means. The residence requirement may stipulate that the child or young person shall not live with a named person, otherwise it is for the local authority to decide where to accommodate him, and the normal regulations for the arrangement of placements, review of cases and applications for the use of secure accommodation apply (Children and Young Persons Act 1969, Section 12, as amended by Children Act 1989, Schedule 12).

- The court may certify that supervision orders which include specified activities requirements are being used instead of custodial sentences, and must state so in open court and that it is satisfied that one of the following criteria applies:
  - that the offender has a history of failure to respond to and is unable or unwilling to respond to other non-custodial penalties
  - that the order is necessary to protect the public from serious harm
  - that the offence was so serious that no other non-custodial sentence can be justified

  and the effect of orders being so certified is that a wider range of sanctions is available if the orders are breached (see below) (Children and Young Persons Act 1969, Section 12, as amended by Criminal Justice Act 1988, Schedule 10).

- On application of the supervisor or the person being supervised, the court may discharge a supervision order or vary it by cancelling or inserting any requirement, but no variation can be made to insert a medical treatment requirement or night restriction requirement after a period of three months has elapsed since the making of the order. (Children and Young Persons Act 1969, Section 15, as amended by Criminal Justice Act 1991, Schedule 7)

- If the person being supervised has not yet reached the age of eighteen and it is proved to the satisfaction of the youth court, on the application of the supervisor, that the person has failed to comply with any requirement, the court may

  - order payment of a fine not exceeding £1,000 (Level 3 offence - see 2.5.4 below)

  - make an attendance centre order

  whether or not it discharges or varies the order (Children and Young Persons Act 1969, Section 15, as amended by Criminal Justice Act 1991, Schedule 7).

- If the person being supervised is eighteen or over and it is proved to the satisfaction of the magistrates' court, on the application of the supervisor, that the person has failed to comply with any requirement, the court may

  - make an order imposing any punishment, other than detention in a young offender institution, which it could have imposed for the original offence

  if it also discharges the supervision order (Children and Young Persons Act 1969, Section 15, as amended by Criminal Justice Act 1991, Schedule 7).

- If the person being supervised is of any age and it is proved to the satisfaction of the relevant court that the person has failed to comply with any requirement directing him to participate in specified activities which the court stated were being imposed instead of a custodial sentence, the court may

  - make an order imposing any sentence which it could have imposed for the original offence

  if it also discharges the supervision order (Children and Young Persons Act 1969, Section 15, as amended by Criminal Justice Act 1991, Schedule 7)

- A supervision order with additional requirements is a community sentence to which the community sentence threshold of offence seriousness, introduced by the

Criminal Justice Act 1991, applies and for which a pre-sentence report is mandatory (see below, paragraph 2.5.5).

### 1.6.6 Attendance Centre Order

- For offenders under twenty-one years of age convicted of an 'imprisonable offence', an attendance centre order may be made of not less than 12 hours or more than 24 hours (where the offender is under sixteen) or more than 36 hours (where the offender is under twenty-one but not less than sixteen). However, in respect of children under fourteen years the court may make an order of less than 12 hours if it is of opinion that 12 hours would be excessive (Criminal Justice Act 1982, Section 17, as amended by Criminal Justice Act 1991, Section 67)

- Where an offender fails to attend in accordance with the order or while attending commits a breach of the attendance centre rules, and this is proven to the satisfaction of the court, the court may

  - order payment of a fine not exceeding £1,000 (Level 3) without prejudice to the continuation of the order.

  - revoke the order and deal with the offender in any way in which it could have dealt with him for the original offence.

  (Criminal Justice Act 1982, Section 19, as amended by Criminal Justice Act 1991, Section 67)

- An attendance centre order is a community sentence for which the community sentence threshold of offence seriousness, introduced by the Criminal Justice Act 1991 applies (see below, paragraph 2.5.5).

### 1.6.7 Curfew Order

- where a person of or over the age of sixteen years is convicted of an offence, for which sentence is not fixed by law, the court may make a curfew order requiring him to remain, for periods specified in the order, at a place specified (Criminal Justice Act 1991, Section 12(1)).

- The curfew order may specify different places or different periods for different days, but must not fall outside a period of six months from the making of the order, or specify periods of less than 2 or more than 12 hours in any one day (Criminal Justice Act 1991, Section 12(2)).

- The requirements in a curfew order must, as far as practicable, be such as to avoid conflict with the offender's religious beliefs, or with the requirements of any other community order to which he may be subject, and interference with times he normally works or attends for education (Criminal Justice Act 1991, Section 12(3)).

- The court must explain the effect of the order and shall not make it unless the offender expresses his willingness to comply with its requirements; and before making the order the court must obtain and consider information about the place proposed to be specified in the order, including information as to the attitude of persons likely to be affected by the enforced presence of the offender (Criminal Justice Act 1991, Section 12(5) and (6)).

- A curfew order may in addition include requirements for securing the electronic monitoring of the offender's whereabouts (Criminal Justice Act 1991, Section 13(1).

- For breach, revocation and amendment of curfew orders, see below (paragraph 2.5.5).

- A curfew order is a community sentence to which the Aommunity sentence threshold of offence seriousness, introduced by the Criminal Justice Act 1991, applies (see below paragraph 2.5.5).

### 1.6.8 Probation Order

- Where a person of or over the age of sixteen years is convicted of an offence, for which sentence is not fixed by law, and the court is of the opinion that supervision by a probation officer is desirable in the interests of

  – securing the rehabilitation of the offender, or

– protecting the public from harm from him or preventing the commission by him of further offences

the court may make a probation order for a period of not less than six months nor more than three years (Powers of Criminal Courts Act 1973, Section 2, as amended by Criminal Justice Act 1991, Section 8).

- The court must explain the effect of the order and shall not make it unless the offender expresses his willingness to comply with its requirements (Powers of Criminal Courts Act 1973, Section 2, as amended by Criminal Justice Act 1991, Section 8).

- An offender in respect of whom a probation order is made shall keep in touch with the probation officer responsible for his supervision in accordance with such instructions as he may from time to time be given and shall notify him of any change of address (Powers of Criminal Courts Act 1973, Section 2, as amended by Criminal Justice Act 1991, Section 8).

- These standard requirements also traditionally include the requirements that the offender be of good behaviour and lead an industrious life, notify any change of employment, and receive visits from the probation officer at home.

- Any other requirements, which, having regard to the circumstances of the case, the court considers desirable, in the interests of securing rehabilitation or protecting the public, may be included in a probation order (Powers of Criminal Courts Act 1973, Section 3(1), as introduced by Criminal Justice Act 1991, Section 9).

- A probation order may include requirements as to the residence of the offender in an approved hostel or any other institution, the period for which must be specified in the order (Powers of Criminal Courts Act 1973, Schedule 1A, as inserted by Criminal Justice Act 1991, Schedule 1).

185

- A probation order may require the offender to present himself to a person or persons at a place or places specified to participate or refrain from participating in activities for not more than 60 days in aggregate and while participating to comply with instructions given by the person in charge of the activities (Powers of Criminal Courts Act 1973, Schedule 1A, as inserted by Criminal Justice Act 1991, Schedule 1).

- A probation order may require the offender to attend at a probation centre on not more than 60 days and, while attending, to comply with instructions given by the person in charge of the centre (Powers of Criminal Courts Act 1973, Schedule 1A, as inserted by Criminal Justice Act 1991, Schedule 1).

- An offender who has been convicted of a sexual offence (defined in Section 31(1) of the Criminal Justice Act 1991) may be required to participate in activities or attend a probation centre for more than 60 days (Powers of Criminal Courts Act 1973, Schedule 1A, as inserted by Criminal Justice Act 1991, Schedule 1).

- Where a court proposing to make a probation order is satisfied, on the evidence of a duly qualified medical practitioner, that the offender's mental condition is such as requires and may be susceptible to treatment (but is not such as to warrant a hospital order or guardianship order), the probation order may include a requirement that the offender submit to treatment

  - as a resident patient in a mental hospital

  - as a non-resident patient at such institution or place specified in the order

  - by or under the direction of a specified duly qualified medical practitioner.

  (Powers of Criminal Courts Act 1973, Schedule 1A, as inserted by Criminal Justice Act 1991, Schedule 1)

- Where a court proposing to make a probation order is satisfied that the offender is dependent on drugs or alcohol, that this dependency caused or contributed to the offence, and his dependency is such as requires and may be susceptible to treatment, the probation order may include a requirement that the offender submit to treatment by or under the direction of a person having the necessary qualifications or experience

  – as a resident in such institution or place as may be specified

  – as a non-resident in or at such institution or place as may be specified

  – by or under the direction of the person specified.

  (Powers of Criminal Courts Act 1973, Schedule 1A, as inserted by Criminal Justice Act 1991, Schedule 1)

- For breach, revocation and amendment of probation orders, see below (paragraph 2.5.5).

- A probation order with additional requirements is a community sentence to which the community sentence threshold of offence seriousness, introduced by the Criminal Justice Act 1991, applies, and for which a pre-sentence report is mandatory (see below paragraph 2.5.5).

### 1.6.9 Community Service Order

- Where a person of sixteen years or over is convicted of an offence punishable with imprisonment (for which sentence is not fixed by law), the court may order the offender to undertake unpaid work of service to the community of not less than forty nor more than two hundred and forty hours (Powers of Criminal Courts Act 1973, Section 14(1), as amended by Criminal Justice Act 1991, Section 10).

- The court shall not make a community service order unless the offender consents and the court, after hearing (if the court thinks it necessary) a probation officer or social worker of a local authority social services department, is satisfied that the offender is a suitable person to perform work under such an order, and provision exists (Powers of Criminal Courts Act 1973, Section 2 and 2A, as amended by Criminal Justice Act 1991, Section 10(3)).

- A person subject to a community service order shall report to the relevant officer and subsequently notify him of any change of address and perform for the number of hours specified in the order such work at such times as he may be instructed by the relevant officer (Powers of Criminal Courts Act 1973, Section 15(1)).

- The instructions given by the relevant officer shall, so far as is practicable, be such as to avoid any conflict with the offender's religious beliefs and any interference with times he normally works or attends for education (Powers of Criminal Courts Act 1973, Section 15(3)).

- The work shall be performed during the period of twelve months beginning with the date of the order, but unless revoked, the order shall remain in force until the offender has worked under it for the number of hours specified (Powers of Criminal Courts Act 1973, Section 15(2), as amended by Criminal Law Act 1977, Schedule 12, Paragraph 4).

- For breach, revocation and amendment of community service orders, see below (paragraph 2.5.5).

- A community service order is a community sentence to which the community sentence threshold of offence seriousness, introduced by the Criminal Justice Act 1991, applies, and for which a pre-sentence report is mandatory (see below, paragraph 2.5.5).

### 1.6.10 Combination Order

- Where a person over the age of sixteen years is convicted of an offence punishable with imprisonment (for which sentence is not fixed by law) the court may make a combination order requiring him both

- To be under the supervision of a probation officer for a period of not less than twelve months nor more than three years; and

- To perform unpaid work for a number of hours so specified being in aggregate not less than 40 nor more than 100.

(Criminal Justice Act 1991, Section 11(1))

- When imposing a combination order, the court must comply with all the procedural requirements necessary for both probation orders and community service orders.

- For breach, revocation and amendment of combination orders, see below (paragraph 2.5.5).

- A combination order is a community sentence to which the community sentence threshold of offence seriousness, introduced by the Criminal Justice Act 1991, applies, and for which a pre-sentence report is mandatory (see below, paragraph 2.5.5).

### 1.6.11 Compensation Order

- Any person found guilty of an offence can be ordered to pay compensation to the victim for any personal injury, loss or damage resulting from the offence. The order can either stand alone or be in addition to any other order made by the court, but where the court considers it appropriate to impose both a fine and a compensation order but the offender has insufficient means, preference must be given to compensation (Powers of Criminal Courts Act 1973, Section 35 as amended by Criminal Justice Act 1982 Section 67).

- The maximum compensation order which may be ordered by a magistrates' court is £5,000 (Magistrates' Courts Act 1980, Section 40(1), as amended by Criminal Justice Act 1991, Section 17(3) and Schedule 4).

- The responsibility of parents and local authorities for compensation orders imposed on young offenders is the same as for fines, described in paragraph 1.6.4 above.

### 1.6.12 Detention in a Young Offender Institution

- Young offenders aged fifteen to twenty years may be sentenced to detention in a young offender institution (Criminal Justice Act 1982, Section 1A(1), as amended by Criminal Justice Act 1991, Section 63(1)).

- The maximum term is the same as the maximum term of imprisonment available for the offence of which the offender has been convicted, subject to a maximum of 12 months for offenders aged fifteen, sixteen or seventeen (Criminal Justice Act 1982, Section 1B(2), as amended by Criminal Justice Act 1991, Section 63(3)).

- The minimum term is 21 days in the case of an offender aged eighteen to twenty years, or 2 months in the case of an offender who is under eighteen years (Criminal Justice Act 1982, Section 1A(2), (3) and (4), as amended by Criminal Justice Act 1991, Section 63(2)).

- The criteria for the imposition of custody and for determining the length of custody are the same as for adult offenders (see below, paragraph 2.5.7).

- An offender aged eighteen to twenty years may be sentenced to custody for life in respect of an offence for which a sentence of life imprisonment is available for an adult offender (Criminal Justice Act 1982, Section 8(2), as amended by Criminal Justice Act 1991, Section 63(5)).

- Young offenders aged eighteen to twenty years may be detained in respect of default of payment of a fine or other sum of money or for contempt of court, but a magistrates' court must state in open court the reason for its opinion that no other method of dealing with the offender is appropriate and enter it in the register (Criminal Justice Act 1982, Section 9, as amended by Criminal Justice Act 1991, Section 63(5) and Schedule 11, Paragraph 30).

- Young offenders aged ten to seventeen years convicted of certain grave offences, namely those punishable with imprisonment of 14 years or over, can be detained up to

190

the maximum that could have been imposed on an adult or 'during Her Majesty's pleasure' for crimes which carry a life sentence. Indecent assault on a woman is to be regarded as a qualifying offence even though the current maximum is 10 years imprisonment (Children and Young Persons Act 1933, Section 53, as amended by Criminal Justice Act 1991, Section 64).

- Where a person under the age of twenty-two years is released from a term of detention in a young offender institution or under Section 53 of the 1933 Act (see above), he shall be under the supervision of a probation officer or a social worker of a local authority social services department, as follows:

  - supervision ends on the offender's twenty-second birthday if it has not ended before

  - unless released on licence (as for adult offenders, see below), the supervision period ends three months from his release

  - where the offender is released on licence and the licence expires less than three months from his release, the supervision period begins on the expiry of the licence and ends three months from his release

  - while under supervision he must comply with such requirements as specified in a notice from the Secretary of State

  - if, without reasonable excuse, he fails to comply with a requirement of supervision, he shall be liable to a fine not exceeding £1,000 (level 3 of the standard scale), or a custodial sentence not exceeding 30 days (which does not render him liable to a further period of supervision but does not prejudice any unexpired period of supervision) (Criminal Justice Act 1991, Section 65).

### 1.6.13 Hospital Orders and Guardianship

- See below, for mentally disordered offenders

## 2. Adult Offenders

### 2.1 Crime Prevention and Discontinuance of Prosecution

2.1.1 Crime prevention is headed nationally by a Ministerial Group on Crime Prevention, which emphasises a crime prevention strategy involving the whole community. Government Circular 44/90 "Crime Prevention: the Success of the Partnership Approach" was accompanied by a booklet 'Partnership in Crime Prevention' (10) giving guidance on successful crime prevention schemes. As part of its contribution, the Home Office has established a 'Safer Cities' programme, with the aims of reducing crime, lessening the fear of crime and creating safer cities within which economic enterprise and community life can flourish. An independent working group, established by the Home Office, has monitored the progress made in the local delivery of crime prevention through the partnership approach, and reported its findings in "Safer Communities" (HMSO 1991).

2.1.2 A registered charity, the Crime Concern Trust Limited, was launched in 1988 with initial funding from the Home Office, using the working title 'Crime Concern' with a central aim of stimulating, supporting and developing effective local crime prevention activities.

2.1.3 The Crown Prosecution Service must assess in each case the merits of the prosecution, using criteria contained in the Code for Crown Prosecutors. The code directs that, after a prosecutor has determined that the evidence in the case presents a realistic prospect of conviction, the Crown Prosecutor must then consider whether the public interest requires a prosecution. The code lists a number of factors which indicate that proceedings may not be in the public interest. Prosecutors are advised to weigh the costs of contemplated proceedings against the likelihood of a nominal penalty being imposed, to give careful consideration to avoiding prosecutions in the cases of young adults, to approach cases of older or infirm dependents with the same reluctance to prosecute and to consider the likelihood that a defendant's mental health may be severely and inappropriately affected by the stress of criminal proceedings. Where doubts remain, the attitude of the local community is also to be considered. To assist the Crown Prosecution Service with information as to its decision making on these public interest criteria, pilot schemes have been established by some Probation Services, commonly called discontinuance schemes or public interest case assessment.

## 2.2 Meaning of Adult Offender

2.2.1 As has been seen above, special sentencing powers and procedures apply to children and young persons under the age of eighteen and to young offenders aged under twenty-one. Persons under twenty-one cannot be sentenced to imprisonment as such; otherwise the normal 'adult' disposals are available for those aged eighteen to twenty, who appear in the 'adult' courts.

2.2.2 There is no specific legal definition of adult offender, other than the fact that special powers and procedures cease to apply to anyone aged twenty-one or over. The confusion comes more in respect of young people with the various terms used, such as

- child (under fourteen)
- young person (aged fourteen to seventeen inclusive)
- youth court (under eighteen)
- young offender (under twenty-one)
- young offender institution (for those under twenty-one)

The Criminal Justice Act 1991 will largely remove the term 'juvenile' by changing the juvenile court to 'youth court', but the everyday language of 'young adult offenders' and 'adult courts' is likely to continue. It is the nature of the procedures and sentencing options which distinguish the differences, and they deliberately overlap, because the "Government considers that sixteen and seventeen year-olds should be dealt with as near adults" and "since some sixteen and seventeen year-olds are more mature than others, the Government believes that there should be some flexibility in the sentencing arrangements for this age group." (11)

2.2.3 For the purpose of this section of this book, therefore, emphasis will be laid on those procedures relating to people aged eighteen and over, and to sentencing options relating to those aged twenty-one and over. Reference back to sentencing options which cover the wider age range will be made, as these have been detailed in the section on young offenders. The overriding principles for custodial sentences, community sentences and financial orders are set out in this section, and relate back to those discussed in the previous section where the emphasis was on particular features relating to young offenders. The scheme for parole, and early release is set out in full in this section, as it relates to both adult offenders and young offenders.

## 2.3 Detention, Treatment and Questioning of Adults by Police

2.3.1 While it may be a social duty to help police with their inquiries, there is no legal obligation to do so. Any person attending a police station voluntarily for the purpose of assisting with an investigation may leave at will unless placed under arrest. (12)

2.3.2 As soon as a suspect is detained, he must be told why and told of his other rights. These are

- the right to see a solicitor,
- the right to have someone told of his detention, and
- the right to see the Code of Practice that the police should follow.

The Code of Practice (13) sets out the conditions and rules which the police should follow when conducting an interrogation, which include the provision of one main meal and two light meals each day; a suspect should be allowed at least eight hours rest each day; a suspect should not be made to stand; there must be a break from interviewing at normal meal times and short refreshments breaks every two hours; the interview room must be properly heated; and rules apply to the tape recording of interviews.

2.3.3 All decisions concerning detention and charge are made by a police officer called the 'custody officer' who must be independent of the investigation into the offence. The police may hold an arrested suspect before charge for up to 24 hours from time of arrival at the police station for the purpose of obtaining evidence. At the end of that period he should be charged or released. If, however, the offence is a 'serious' one, a senior police officer can authorise detention up to 36 hours. At the end of that time the police can ask a magistrates' court to allow further detention without charge for a further 36 hours, to a maximum of 96 hours. This court hearing is in private, and friends and relatives cannot attend, but the suspect's solicitor can (Police and Criminal Evidence Act 1984, Part IV).

2.3.4 Having arrested and charged a suspect, whether or not to grant police bail is entirely a matter of the police's discretion. If police bail is granted, the person charged will be notified of when and where to present himself for trial. If police bail is refused, the prisoner must be brought before a magistrate within 24 hours. This is extended to 48 hours at weekends and bank holidays (Police and Criminal Evidence Act 1984, Sections 46 and 47).

## 2.4 Adult Remands

2.4.1 The Bail Act 1976 guarantees a right to bail to every person charged with a criminal offence unless one of several strict legal exceptions apply. Exceptions are known as 'grounds', and magistrates must state which grounds apply and support this with reasons. Grounds vary according to whether or not the offence is imprisonable. Briefly, grounds can be:

- for all offences
  - arrested for breach of bail.
  - held in custody for own protection.
  - already in custody.

- for imprisonable offences

  - grounds for believing the defendant would fail to surrender to custody.

  - grounds for believing the defendant would commit an offence.

  - grounds for believing the defendant would interfere with witnesses.

  - it has been impracticable to get information.

2.4.2 Increasingly probation services have been introducing Bail Information Schemes to assist courts with decisions in respect of bail and remands in custody.

2.4.3 If the magistrate decides to remand a defendant in custody the maximum is a remand for eight clear days, unless the court has previously remanded him in custody for the same offence and he is before the court, but only if it has set a date on which it will be possible for the next stage in the proceedings to take place and then only for a period ending not later than that date or for 28 days whichever is the less (Magistrates' Courts Act 1980, Section 128, as amended by Criminal Justice Act 1988, Section 155).

2.4.4 There are limits on the total length of time for which a defendant may be held in custody before a case is started. Cases triable either summarily or on indictment ('either way' offences) which are to be tried by the magistrates' court must be started within 70 days or a shorter period of 56 days if mode of trial has been decided within 56 days. If a case is committed for trial, the committal process must begin within 70 days. A period of 112 days is allowed between the date when magistrates commit the defendant to the Crown Court and his appearance there for the indictment to be read. If a time limit expires, the defendant cannot be remanded in custody any longer. He may still be prosecuted but must be released on bail pending the hearing (Prosecution of Offences Act 1985, Section 22).

## 2.5 Sentencing Options in the Adult Courts

### 2.5.1 Deferment of Sentence

- See above, paragraph 1.6.1.

### 2.5.2 Bind Over

- Magistrates have an ancient power to bind over a person to be of good behaviour and to keep the peace. It is a form of preventive justice, as it acts to prevent future trouble rather than punish for past misbehaviour. The defendant enters into a 'recognisance' or undertaking to behave for a period fixed by the court – usually 12 months – or risks forfeiting a sum of money set by the court. Bind overs can be made on the application of an individual, often a private individual, or of the court's own motion. Modern provisions regulate procedure and applications by individuals. The power to bind over can be used on its own or in addition to any penalty (Justices of the Peace Act 1361, and Courts Act 1971 and Magistrates' Courts Act 1980, Section 115 and Section 116).

### 2.5.3 Absolute Discharge and Conditional Discharge

- See above, paragraph 1.6.3.

### 2.5.4 Fine

- Where an offender has been convicted in a magistrates' court of an offence triable 'either way', the maximum fine is £5,000 (Criminal Justice Act 1991, Section 17(2)).

- Fines imposed by magistrates' courts (with three exceptions) are determined by a system of unit fines:

  - The fine is a product of the number of units which is determined by the court to be commensurate with the seriousness of the offence or offences and the value to be ascribed to each of those units in accordance with rules which show the offender's disposable weekly income.

  - The court first determines the number of units appropriate to the seriousness of the case within maxima which are tied to the standard scale of fines, as follows

Level 1 offence     2 units

Level 2 offence     5 units

Level 3 offence     10 units

Level 4 offence     25 units

Level 5 offences    50 units

(Criminal Justice Act 1991, Section 18(1), (2), (3) and (4))

- In no case shall the value of a unit exceed £100 and in no case shall the value of a unit fall below £4; thus the maximum fine available is level 5:

$$50 \text{ units} \times £100 = £5,000$$

which is the maximum for a magistrates' court (Criminal Justice Act 1991, Section 18(5)).

- For offenders under the age of fourteen, the value of a unit shall be not less than 20 pence nor more than £5, producing a maximum of £250, and for offenders aged fourteen to seventeen years the value of a unit shall be not less than 80p nor more than £20, producing a maximum of £1,000 (Criminal Justice Act 1991, Section 18(6)).

- The rules for determining an offender's disposable income are to be drawn up by the Lord Chancellor.

- In determining the number of units to be commensurate with the seriousness of the offence the court is required to take account of any information relating to the circumstances of the offence, including any mitigating or aggravating factors (Criminal Justice Act 1991, Section 18(3)).

- The system of unit fines does not apply to the Crown Court and there are no upper limits for the Crown Courts, but maximum fines are fixed for most statutory offences. The Crown Court has a general power to impose a fine in lieu of or in addition to dealing with an offender in any other way in which it has power to deal with him (Powers of Criminal Courts Act 1973, Section 30).

- The Crown Court can deal with an offender for a summary offence only in a manner in which a magistrates' court could have dealt with him, but this does not mean a unit fine if it chooses to impose a fine (Criminal Justice Act 1988, Section 41(7) and Criminal Justice Act 1991, Section 18(9)).

### 2.5.5 Community Sentence

- A community sentence means

  – a probation order

  – a community service order

  – a combination order

  – a curfew order

  – a supervision order

  – an attendance centre order

  and a court shall not pass a community sentence unless it is of opinion that the offence or the combination of the offence and one other offence associated with it, was serious enough to warrant such a sentence (Criminal Justice Act 1991, Section 6(1) and (4)).

- The court must be of opinion that the particular order or orders is or are the most suitable for the offender and the restrictions on liberty imposed by the order or orders are commensurate with the seriousness of the offence; in forming that opinion the court must take into account information about the circumstances of the offence (including any aggravating or mitigating factors) and any information about the offender available to it. The court must consider a pre-sentence report before forming an opinion as to the suitability of one or more of the following orders:

- a probation order with additional requirements
- a community service order
- a combination order
- a supervision order with additional requirements.

(Criminal Justice Act 1991, Section 6(2) and 7(1), (2) and (3))

• For details of procedural requirements and requirements of the orders in respect of the following, see above:

- probation orders, paragraph 1.6.8
- community service orders, paragraph 1.6.9
- combination orders, paragraph 1.6.10
- curfew orders, paragraph 1.6.7
- supervision orders, paragraph 1.6.5
- attendance centre orders, paragraph 1.6.6.

• Where a person fails without reasonable excuse to comply with a requirement or requirements of

- a probation order
- a community service order
- a curfew order, or
- a combination order

and it is proved to the satisfaction of a magistrates' court, the court may

- impose a fine not exceeding £1,000,
- make a community service order of not more than 60 hours, but where the offender is in breach of a community service order the total number of hours under both orders must not exceed 240,
- where the offender is in breach of a probation order and it is a case where Section 17 of the Criminal Justice Act 1982 applies, make an attendance centre order,

- revoke the order and deal with the offence in respect of which the order was made in any manner in which it could deal with it as if the offender had just been convicted,

- where the original order was made by the Crown Court, commit the offender to the Crown Court, which has identical powers for dealing with breaches as the magistrates' court, except where it revokes the order and deals with the original offence.

(Criminal Justice Act 1991, Schedule 2, Part II)

• A probation order, community service order, curfew order or combination order may be revoked on application of the offender or responsible officer if it appears to the magistrates' court that having regard to circumstances which have arisen since the order was made, it would be in the interests of justice to do so. The magistrates' court may

- revoke the order,

- revoke the order and deal with the original offence in any manner in which it had power to do so,

- if the order was made by the Crown Court, commit the offender to the Crown Court,

and both the magistrates' court and Crown Court, if they deal with the original offence, must take into account the extent to which the offender has complied with the requirements of the relevant order and may assume, in the case of an offender who has wilfully and persistently failed to comply with those requirements, he has refused to give his consent to a community sentence which requires that consent (Criminal Justice Act 1991, Schedule 2, Part II and Part III).

• Community orders may be amended on the application of the relevant officer, normally with the offender's consent, and in his presence (unless it is to cancel or reduce the period of any requirement, or to substitute a new petty sessions area or a new place for one specified in the order). In particular, it should be noted,

- a probation order cannot be amended to reduce the period or to extend it beyond three years,

- a requirement in a probation order that the offender submit to treatment for his mental condition or his dependency on drugs or alcohol, cannot be inserted three months after the date of the original order,

- the medical practitioner or other person responsible must report in writing to the responsible officer any opinion for the extension of treatment, change of treatment or termination of treatment, required under a probation order, and the responsible officer shall then apply for variation or cancellation of the requirement,

- a curfew order cannot be amended to extend beyond six months of the original order,

- a community service order can be extended beyond twelve months if it would be in the interests of justice to do so having regard to the circumstances which have arisen since the order was made.

(Criminal Justice Act 1991, Schedule 2, Part IV)

- Details relating to the breach, revocation and amendment of other community sentences are given above, as follows

- supervision orders, paragraph 1.6.5.

- attendance centre orders, paragraph, 1.6.6.

- National standards governing the planning, supervision, enforcement and management of Community Service Order by the Probation Service are set out in Home Office Circular 18/1989; national standards in respect of probation orders, probation programmes, combination orders and approved hostels are also being developed.

### 2.5.6  Compensation Order

- For details of compensation orders, see above, at paragraph 1.6.11.

- Additionally it should be noted that in a curious and controversial provision of the Criminal Justice Act 1991, the Secretary of State is empowered to draw up regulations to provide for the deduction from an offender's income support, payments of certain sums in respect of a fine or compensation order imposed by a magistrates' court, but not by the Crown Court.

(Criminal Justice Act 1991, Section 24)

### 2.5.7 Custodial Sentences

- Custodial sentence means in relation to an offender of or over the age of twenty-one years, a sentence of imprisonment, and in relation to an offender under that age, a sentence of detention in a young offender institution or under Section 53 of the Children and Young Persons Act 1933 or a sentence of custody for life (Criminal Justice Act 1991, Section 31(1)).

- A court (either Crown Court or magistrates' court) shall not pass a custodial sentence on the offender, other than one fixed by law, unless it is of opinion

  - that the offence, or the combination of the offence and one other offence associated with it, was so serious that only such a sentence can be justified; or

  - where the offence is a violent or sexual offence, that only such a sentence would be adequate to protect the public from serious harm from him

  but this shall not prevent the court from passing a custodial sentence if the offender refuses to give his consent to a community sentence which is proposed by the court and requires that consent (Criminal Justice Act 1991, Section 1(1), (2) and (3)).

- The court is obliged to state in open court and in ordinary language why it is of opinion that the 'seriousness' or 'public protection' criterion apply to the case, and a magistrates' court must enter it in the register (Criminal Justice Act 1991, Section 1(4))

- The custodial sentence shall be for such terms (not exceeding the permitted maximum) as in the opinion of the court is commensurate with the seriousness of the offence or offences, or if a violent or sexual offence, for such term (not exceeding the maximum) as is necessary to protect the public from serious harm from the offender; before forming its opinion the court must obtain and consider a pre-sentence report and in forming its opinion take into account all such information about the circumstances of the offence (including any aggravating or mitigating factors) and any information about the offender (Criminal Justice Act 1991, Section 2(1), 3(1) and (3)).

- An offence shall not be regarded as more serious by reason of any previous convictions or any failure to respond to previous sentences, but where any aggravating factors of an offence are disclosed by the circumstances of other offences committed by the offender, those factors may be taken into account for the purpose of forming an opinion as to the seriousness of the offence (Criminal Justice Act 1991, Section 29(1) and (2)).

- A sentence of imprisonment of not more than two years may be suspended for an 'operational period' of not less than one year or more than two years, if the court is of opinion that imprisonment is appropriate but the exercise of that power can be justified by the exceptional circumstances of the case. The court must consider, when passing a suspended sentence, whether the case warrants in addition the imposition of a fine or compensation order. The same procedural requirements apply to suspended sentences as to immediate custody (Powers of Criminal Courts Act 1973, Section 22, as amended by Criminal Justice Act 1991, Section 5).

- Where the Crown Court passes on an offender a suspended sentence for a term of more than six months the court may make a suspended sentence supervision order for a specified period, being a period not exceeding the operational period, placing the offender under the supervision of a probation officer (Powers of Criminal Courts Act 1973, Section 26).

### 2.5.8 Hospital Orders and Guardianship

- See below, for mentally disordered offenders.

## 2.6 Parole and Early Release of Prisoners

2.6.1 As soon as a short-term prisoner (i.e. a person serving a term of less than four years) has served one-half of his sentence he must be

- released unconditionally if his sentence is for a term less than twelve months
- released on licence if his sentence is for a term of twelve months or more

and, if subject to licence, the licence will expire (and the release become unconditional) on the date on which he would (but for his release) have served three-quarters of his sentence (Criminal Justice Act 1991, Section 33(1) and (5) and 37(1)).

2.6.2 A long-term prisoner (i.e. a person serving a term of four years or more)

- must be released as soon as he has served two-thirds of his sentence.
- or after he has served one-half of his sentence, the Secretary of State may, if recommended to do so by the Parole Board, release him on licence,

and, if subject to licence, the licence will remain in force until the date on which he would (but for his release) have served three-quarters of his sentence) (Criminal Justice Act 1991, Section 33(2) and (5) and 37(1)).

2.6.3 Life sentence prisoners are of two kinds

- *mandatory* (i.e. those sentenced to life imprisonment for murder) who may be released on licence at any time if recommended by the Parole Board, after consultation with the Lord Chief Justice and the trial judge, if available;

205

- *discretionary* (i.e. those sentenced to life imprisonment for violent or sexual offences, the sentence for which is not fixed by law and the court which sentenced him ordered that as soon as he had served a specified part of his sentence he could be considered for release on licence) who must be released on licence if the Parole Board directs it, having satisfied itself that it is no longer necessary for the protection of the public that he be confined,

and the licence for life sentence prisoners, unless revoked, remains in force until their death (Criminal Justice Act 1991, Section 34(1), (3), (4), 35(2) and 37(3)).

2.6.4 Failure by a short-term prisoner to comply with the conditions of a licence is a summary offence punishable by a unit fine not exceeding level 3 (£1,000), but the magistrates' court may also

- suspend the licence for a period not exceeding six months and order recall to prison for the period during which the licence is suspended.

(Criminal Justice Act 1991, Section 38(1) and (2)).

2.6.5 A long-term or life prisoner may have his licence revoked and be recalled to prison by the Secretary of State if recommended to do so by the Parole Board, or without such a recommendation where it appears expedient in the public interest to recall the person before such a recommendation is practicable (Criminal Justice Act 1991, Section 39(1) and (2)).

2.6.6 A discretionary life prisoner refused release on licence after the specified period can require his case to be referred to the Parole Board at intervals of two years. A long-term or life prisoner whose licence is revoked and he is recalled to prison may make representations and have his case referred to the Parole Board, and must be released if recommended by Parole Board (Criminal Justice Act 1991, Section 34(5) and 39(3), (4) and (5)).

2.6.7 Any additional days awarded to a prisoner for disciplinary offences under the Prison Rules are added to the period which he must serve before becoming entitled to or eligible for release under the provision for early release (Criminal Justice Act 1991, Section 42).

2.6.8 Supervision on licence is by a probation officer, or, in the case of a young offender, it may be by a local authority social worker, and the Secretary of State may make rules for regulating the supervision (Criminal Justice Act 1991, Section 37(4) and 43(5)).

## 3. Mentally Disordered Offenders

### 3.1 The Detention, Treatment and Questioning of Mentally Ill or Mentally Handicapped Persons

3.1.1 The law in respect of the detention, treatment and questioning of persons by the police is set out above in paragraph 2.3, but there are particular provisions in the Code of Practice (5) relating to people who may be mentally ill or mentally handicapped.

3.1.2 If an officer has any suspicion, or is told in good faith, that a person of any age may be mentally ill or mentally handicapped, or mentally incapable of understanding the significance of questions put to him or his replies, then that person shall be treated as a mentally ill or mentally handicapped person for the purposes of the code (14).

3.1.3 A mentally ill or mentally handicapped person must not be interviewed or asked to provide or sign a written statement in the absence of an appropriate adult, unless and only if an officer of the rank of superintendent or above considers that delay will involve an immediate risk of harm to persons or serious loss of or serious damage to property (15).

3.1.4 In the case of a person who is mentally ill or mentally handicapped appropriate adult means

- a relative, guardian or other person responsible for his care or custody;

- someone who has experience of dealing with mentally ill or mentally handicapped persons but is not a police officer or employed by the police; or

- failing either of the above, some other responsible adult who is not a police officer or employed by the police (16).

3.1.5  The custody officer must immediately call the police surgeon (or, in urgent cases, send the person to hospital or call the nearest available medical practitioner) if a person brought to a police station or already detained there appears to be suffering from mental illness (17).

3.1.6  A summary of all the provisions relating to mentally ill and mentally handicapped persons is given in Annex E of Code C of the Codes of Practice.

## 3.2 Fitness to Stand Trial

3.2.1  As noted above, at paragraph 2.1.3, the Crown Prosecution Service, in considering whether the public interest requires a prosecution, should consider the likelihood that a defendant's mental health may be severely and inappropriately affected by the stress of criminal proceedings. Discontinuance schemes may give particular attention to mentally disordered people.

3.2.2  It is generally accepted that people are to be held responsible for their actions, but there is a long legal history of insanity being a defence, and it is possible for a court to return a 'special verdict' of not guilty by reason of insanity, for which there is a mandatory disposal of detention in hospital under the Criminal Procedure (Insanity) Act 1964, which has the same effect as a restriction order without limit of time imposed under Section 41 of the Mental Health Act 1983 (see below). A special verdict relates to cases where the defendant was very seriously mentally disordered at the time of committing the offence.

3.2.3  If the accused is suffering from mental disorder at the time of trial it may be held that he is 'unfit to plead' or 'under disability in relation to the trial'. By tradition, a court has

208

to be satisfied that an accused person can understand the charges against him, exercise his right to challenge a juror, follow the evidence and instruct counsel. If an accused is not able to do so, he will customarily be held to be 'under disability', and detained under the Criminal Procedure (Insanity) Act 1964, Section 4, which has the same effect as a restriction order under the Mental Health Act 1983, Section 41 (see below).

3.2.4 New legislation, the Criminal Procedure (Insanity and Unfitness to Plead) Act 1991 amends the law relating to the special verdict and unfitness to plead by substituting a new Section 4 for that in the 1964 Act. It also provides for a trial of the facts in cases of defendants found to be unfit to plead. But most significantly it increases the powers of the Crown Court and Appeal Court in the event of defendants being found to be insane or unfit to plead, by adding to the power to make an order for admission to hospital, the power to make one of the following orders they think most suitable in all the circumstances:

- a guardianship order within the meaning of the Mental Health Act 1983,

- a supervision and treatment order, which requires the person to be under the supervision of a social worker or probation officer and to submit to treatment, for a specified period of not more than two years,

- an order for absolute discharge,

unless the offence is one for which the sentence is fixed by law.

This new legislation is yet to be implemented.

## 3.3 Remands to Hospital

3.3.1 The Crown Court or magistrates' court may remand an accused person to a hospital specified by the court for a report on his mental condition, if

- awaiting trial before a Crown Court but not yet sentenced for an offence punishable with imprisonment,

209

- convicted by a magistrates' court of an offence punishable with imprisonment or charged with such an offence and the court is satisfied the person committed the offence, or the person consents to the remand,

and a duly authorised medical practitioner has given written or oral evidence that there is reason to believe that the accused is suffering from mental illness, psychopathic disorder, severe mental impairment, or mental impairment and the court is satisfied that it would be impracticable for a report on his mental condition to be made if he were remanded on bail. Admission to hospital must be within seven days of the remand. The initial remand may be for up to twenty-eight days, with further remands of up to twenty-eight days to a maximum of twelve weeks (Mental Health Act 1983, Section 35(1), (2), (3) and (6)).

3.3.2 The Crown Court may remand an accused person to hospital for treatment, if satisfied on the written or oral evidence of two authorised medical practitioners that the accused is suffering from mental illness or severe mental impairment of a nature or degree which makes it appropriate for him to be detained in hospital for medical treatment.

Admission to hospital must be within seven days of the remand. The initial remand may be for up to twenty-eight days, with further remands of up to twenty-eight days up to a maximum of twelve weeks. (Mental Health Act 1983, Section 36(1), (3) and (6)).

3.3.3 A person remanded to hospital may obtain an independent medical report at his own expense and apply to the court on the basis of that report to have his remand ended (Mental Health Act 1983, Section 35(8) and 36(7)).

## 3.4 Interim Hospital Order

3.4.1 The Crown Court or magistrates' court may make a interim hospital order in respect of an offender convicted of an offence, other than murder, punishable with imprisonment, if satisfied, on the written or oral evidence of two authorised medical practitioners that:

- the offender is suffering from one of the four specific forms of mental disorder; and

- a hospital order may be appropriate.

(Mental Health Act 1983, Section 38(1))

3.4.2 An interim hospital order may be for a period up to twelve weeks as specified by the court, renewable for periods of twenty-eight days at a time up to a maximum of six months (Mental Health Act 1983, Section 38(5)).

## 3.5 Hospital Order

3.5.1 A Crown Court or magistrates' court may, in respect of a person convicted of an offence, other than murder, punishable with imprisonment, make a hospital order if:

- satisfied on the evidence of two medical practitioners, one of whom must be approved, that the offender is suffering from one of the four specific forms of mental disorder of a nature or degree which warrants detention in hospital for treatment;

- in the case of psychopathic disorder and mental impairment, that treatment is likely to alleviate or prevent a deterioration in his condition;

- admission to hospital will be within twenty-eight days;

- both medical practitioners describe the offender as suffering from one of the mental disorders, in common;

- having regard to all the circumstances, the court is satisfied that a hospital order is the most suitable method of dealing with the case.

(Mental Health Act 1983, Section 37(1), (2), (4) and (7))

3.5.2 A magistrates' court may, if the above conditions for a hospital order are met, and it is satisfied that the accused committed the offence and it thinks fit to do so, make a hospital order without convicting him (Mental Health Act 1983, Section 37(3)).

3.5.3 If the Crown Court makes a hospital order and it appears to the court necessary for the protection of the public from serious harm, then the court may make a 'restriction order' without limit of time or for a specified period, under which the patient will be detained unless granted leave of absence or discharge (absolute or conditional) by the Home Secretary (Mental Health Act 1983, Section 41(1) and (3) and Section 42(2) and (3)).

3.5.4 The effect of a hospital order is similar to an admission for treatment under Part II of the Mental Health Act 1983 (see chapter 3) except that the nearest relative has no right to consultation or of discharge (Mental Health Act 1983, Section 40(4) and Schedule 1).

## 3.6 Guardianship Order

3.6.1 The Crown Court and magistrates' court may, in respect of a person convicted of an offence, other than murder, punishable with imprisonment, make a guardianship order if:

- the offender is at least sixteen years of age;

- the court is satisfied on the evidence of two medical practitioners, one of whom must be approved, that the offender is suffering from one of the four specific forms of mental disorder of a nature or degree which warrants guardianship; and

- having regard to all the circumstances the court is satisfied that a guardianship order is the most suitable method of dealing with the case.

(Mental Health Act 1983, Section 37(1) and (2))

3.6.2 A magistrates' court may, if the above conditions for a guardianship order are met, and it is satisfied that the accused committed the offence and if it thinks fit to do so, make a guardianship order without convicting him (Mental Health Act 1983, Section 37(3)).

3.6.3 A guardianship order can only be made if the local authority or nominated guardian is willing to receive the person into guardianship (Mental Health Act 1983, Section 37(6)).

3.6.4 The effect of a guardianship order is similar to admission to guardianship under Part II of the Mental Health Act 1983 (see chapter 3).

## 3.7 Removal to Hospital of Other Prisoners

3.7.1 The Home Secretary is empowered to direct that sentenced prisoners should be removed from prison to hospital if satisfied, by reports from two registered medical practitioners, that they are suffering from one of the four specific forms of mental disorder, and that, having regard to the public interest and all the circumstances, such a transfer is expedient. He is likewise empowered to transfer unconvicted prisoners from prison to hospital if satisfied, as a result of reports from two medical practitioners, that they are suffering from mental illness or severe mental impairment of a nature or degree which makes it appropriate for them to be detained in a mental hospital and they are in urgent need of such treatment (Mental Health Act 1983, Sections 47(1) and 48(1) and (2)).

3.7.2 The prisoner is admitted to the hospital under a Transfer Direction which has the same effect as a Hospital Order (Mental Health Act 1983, Section 47(3)).

3.7.3 Where a transfer direction relates to a person remanded in custody by a magistrates' court, the transfer direction will cease to have effect on the expiry of the period of remand unless the accused is committed in custody to the Crown Court. If the magistrates' court is satisfied on the written or oral evidence of the Responsible Medical Officer that the accused no longer requires hospital treatment, it may end the transfer direction (Mental Health Act 1983, Section 52(1), (2) and (5)).

3.7.4 Where a person serving a sentence of imprisonment is subject to a transfer direction, the Secretary of State may also impose a 'restriction direction', which has the same effect as a restriction order. Where a person remanded in custody is subject to a transfer direction, the Secretary of State must impose a restriction direction. While a person is subject to a restriction direction , the responsible medical officer must examine him and report to the Secretary of State at least once a year (Mental Health Act 1983, Section 49(1), (2) and (3)).

## 3.8 Applications to Mental Health Review Tribunals

3.8.1 An application to a Mental Health Review Tribunal may be made by a patient detained under a hospital order or by the nearest relative. The application can be made after six months and before the completion of twelve months of the order, and again in any subsequent twelve month period (Mental Health Act 1983, Section 69(1)).

3.8.2 An application may be made on behalf of a patient under guardianship either by the patient himself within six months of the beginning of the order, or by the nearest relative within twelve months and in any subsequent twelve month period (Mental Health Act 1983, Section 69(1)).

3.8.3 Restricted patients may apply to a tribunal in the period between the expiry of six months and the expiry of twelve months beginning with the date of the hospital order or transfer direction, and in any subsequent period of twelve months (Mental Health Act 1983, Section 70).

3.8.4 The Secretary of State may refer the case of a restricted patient to a Tribunal at any time, but must refer every case of a restricted patient which has not been considered by a Tribunal within the last three years (Mental Health Act 1983, Section 71(1) and (2)).

3.8.5 The Mental Health Review Tribunal must discharge an unrestricted patient if he is not suffering from one of the specific forms of mental disorder of a nature or degree to warrant detention or if detention is not warranted in the interests of the patient's health or safety or for the protection of others (Mental Health Act 1983, Section 72).

3.8.6 The Mental Health Review Tribunal must order the absolute discharge of a restricted patient if satisfied:

- that the patient is not suffering from a mental disorder or not of a nature or degree which warrants his detention in hospital for treatment; or

- that treatment is not necessary for his own health or safety or for the protection of others; and

- that it is not appropriate for the patient to remain liable to be recalled to hospital for further treatment

and then both the hospital order and the restriction order cease to have effect (Mental Health Act 1983, Section 73(1) and (3)).

3.8.7 If satisfied on the first two grounds above, but not the third, the Mental Health Review Tribunal may order the conditional discharge of a restricted patient, and then he may be recalled to hospital by the Secretary of State and must comply with any conditions imposed at the time of discharge by the Tribunal or subsequently by the Secretary of State, who may, from time to time, vary the imposed conditions. If a restriction order ceases to have effect while a patient is on conditional discharge and he is not recalled to hospital, he will be deemed to be absolutely discharged (Mental Health Act 1983, Section 73(2), (4), (5) and (6)).

3.8.8 If a patient subject to a restriction direction applies or is referred to a Tribunal, the tribunal must inform the Secretary of State whether the patient, if he were under a restriction order, would be entitled to be absolutely or conditionally discharged, and if the recommendation is for conditional discharge, it must also advise if the patient is not discharged whether he should continue to be detained in hospital. If the tribunal recommends absolute discharge or conditional discharge without advising continued detention in hospital, then the Secretary of State must direct the transfer of the patient to prison, whereupon the transfer direction and restriction direction cease to have effect (Mental Health Act 1983, Section 74(1), (4) and (5)).

## 3.9 Aftercare

3.9.1 As was noted in chapter 3, the Mental Health Act imposes a duty on the district health authority and the social services department to provide aftercare services for patients who have been detained for treatment or under a hospital order or those in hospital following a transfer direction, and the duty continues until the two authorities are satisfied that the person no longer needs such a service (Mental Health Act 1983, Section 117(1), (2) and (3)).

3.9.2 When a restricted patient has committed an offence of violence or there is apprehension that he might have dangerous tendencies, the Home Secretary normally prefers that his discharge from hospital is subject to conditions. These often relate to residence at a particular address, supervision by a probation officer or social worker and medical surveillance. The supervising officer should provide support and guidance to the patient and early warning of any relapse in the patient's mental condition or deterioration in behaviour giving rise to danger to himself or others.

3.9.3 The pattern of supervision is at the supervising officer's discretion. A report is provided to the Home Office a month after discharge and then at quarterly intervals, with less frequency if satisfactory resettlement in the community is sustained. The conditions of the Home Secretary's warrant of conditional discharge may be varied at any time if necessary.

3.9.4 A conditionally discharged patient may be recalled to hospital by the Home Secretary and then becomes liable to detention as a restricted patient, but his case must be referred to a Mental Health Review Tribunal by the Home Secretary within one month of re-admission to hospital. Thereafter, the patient's right to apply to a tribunal is that of any restricted patient (see above paragraph 3.8.3). The re-admission date is taken as the admission date (Mental Health Act 1983, Section 75(1)).

3.9.5 Where a restricted patient has been conditionally discharged and has not been recalled to hospital, he may apply to a Mental Health Review Tribunal in the period between expiry of twelve months and two years beginning on the date of the conditional discharge and in any subsequent period of two years, and the tribunal may vary the conditions or direct that the restriction order or restriction direction cease to have effect (Mental Health Act 1983, Section 75(2)).

## 3.10 Probation and Mentally Disordered Offenders

See above, paragraph 1.6.8

## 4. Victims of Crime

### 4.1 Victim Support

Victim support schemes – over 350 in all – cover most of England and Wales, supported by government funds. Police refer victims of offences to local schemes. Particular advice has been given to the police on the treatment of victims of rape and domestic violence, in Home Office Circular 69/1986, and provisions to ensure the anonymity of rape victims from the moment of allegation are contained in the Sexual Offences (Amendment) Act 1976 as amended by Criminal Justice Act 1988, Section 158.

### 4.2 Information for Victims

4.2.1 The Home Office has advised the criminal justice services on improvements in the way victims are dealt with and kept informed, in Home Office Circular 20/1988. It has produced a leaflet called "Victims of Crime", which the police should make available to all victims of crime. This explains how they may be able to claim compensation for injury or loss through the courts or the Criminal Injuries Compensation Board, and how to obtain information about the progress of their cases and about crime prevention.

4.2.2 A second Home Office leaflet called "Witness in Court" explains what is involved in being called to give evidence. Both leaflets are available free from the police and victim support schemes.

### 4.3 The Victim's Charter

The government has issued a Victim's Charter (18) which is a statement of the rights of victims of crime, setting out how they should be treated and what they are entitled to expect. Copies of the charter are available from Room 101, Home Office, 50 Queen Anne's Gate, London, SW1H 9AT.

## 5. Partnership in Dealing with Offenders in the Community

At the same time as it published the White Paper, 'Crime, Justice and Protecting the Public' (1), and the Green Paper, 'Supervision and Punishment in the Community' (2), the Home Office published a Discussion Paper entitled 'Partnership in dealing with offenders in the community' (19). The aim of the paper was to discuss how to build on and develop the work of voluntary organisations and the private sector in the criminal justice system, in partnership with government and the statutory agencies – principally the probation service. The common thread running through the discussion is wider involvement of the community in work with offenders to reduce crime. A debate about the role and funding of the independent sector, the place of volunteers, and their relationship with the statutory agencies is likely to go on as the Criminal Justice Act 1991 is progressively implemented.

## References

1.  Home Office (1990) "Crime, Justice and Protecting the Public", HMSO, Cmnd 965, London.

2.  Home Office (1990) "Supervision and Punishment in the Community: A Framework for Action", HMSO, Cmnd 966, London.

3.  Department of Health (1991) "The Children Act 1989 Guidance and Regulations", Volume 1, Paragraph 6.4.

4.  Department of Health (1991) "The Children Act 1989 Guidance and Regulations", Volume 1, Paragraph 6.5.

5.  Home Office (1991) "Police and Criminal Evidence Act 1984, Section 66, Code of Practice" (Second Edition), HMSO, London, Code C.

6.  Home Office (1991) "Police and Criminal Evidence Act 1984, Section 66, Code of Practice" (Second Edition), HMSO, London, Code C, Paragraph 11.14.

7.  Home Office (1991) "Police and Criminal Evidence Act 1984, Section 66, Code of Practice" (Second Edition), HMSO, London, Code C, Paragraph 1.7.

8.  Home Office (1991) "Police and Criminal Evidence Act 1984, Section 66, Code of Practice" (Second Edition), HMSO, London, Code C, Paragraph 11.16.

9.  Department of Health (1991) "The Children Act 1989 Guidance and Regulations", Volume 7, Paragraph 7.6.

10. Home Office (1990) "Partnership in Crime Prevention", HMSO, London.

11. Home Office (1990) "Crime, Justice and Protecting the Public", HMSO, London, Paragraph 8.16 and 8.17.

12. Home Office (1991) "Police and Criminal Evidence Act 1984, Section 66, Code of Practice" (Second Edition), HMSO, London, Code C, Paragraph 3.9.

13. Home Office (1991) "Police and Criminal Evidence Act 1984, Section 66, Code of Practice" (Second Edition), HMSO, London, Code C.

14. Home Office (1991) "Police and Criminal Evidence Act 1984, Section 66, Code of Practice" (Second Edition), HMSO, London, Code C, Paragraph 1.4.

15. Home Office (1991) "Police and Criminal Evidence Act 1984, Section 66, Code of Practice" (Second Edition), HMSO, London, Code C, Paragraph 11.14.

16. Home Office (1991) "Police and Criminal Evidence Act 1984, Section 66, Code of Practice" (Second Edition), HMSO, London, Code C, Paragraph 1.7.

17. Home Office (1991) "Police and Criminal Evidence Act 1984, Section 66, Code of Practice" (Second Edition), HMSO, London, Code C, Paragraph 9.2.

18. Home Office (1990) "Victim's Charter", HMSO, London.

19. Home Office (1990) "Partnership in dealing with offenders in the Community", Home Office, London.

# Subject Index